.

ARENS, William. On the frontier of change: Mto Wa Mbu, Tanzania. University of Michigan (dist. by University Microfilms International), 1979. 150p (Anthropology series) 79-18843. 10.00 pa ISBN 0-472-02714-X. C.I.P.
More than 80 percent of the 17.5 million Tanzanians have been moved to densely populated communal villages in a process called "villagization." Formerly known as *ujamaa*, the program provides social services at the lowest cost for the maximum number of people. Few studies focusing on the Third World have ignored this East African nation's dynamic social experiment and its consequences for local-level political organization. The polyethnic settlement of Mto Wa Mbu could well serve as a model community for the problem-ridden program. Arens, an anthropologist who wrote *The man-eating myth* (CHOICE, Jul.–Aug. 1979), undertook research in this town of 3,500 and carefully examined how social patterns were formed and reshaped by economical, ecological, and personal factors over several decades. Extensive interviews with residents of many ethnic groups are interwoven with perceptive socioanthropological data to produce a lucid, penetrating study that challenges anthropological assumptions averred in other community studies. Eleven detailed tables and three maps enhance the analysis. By deftly including other rural and urban studies,

Arens has contributed a major work that will be of interest to anthropologists, political scientists, and all interested in development throughout the Third World. Level: advanced undergraduate through professional.

ON THE FRONTIER OF CHANGE

ANTHROPOLOGY SERIES

Series Editor, Vern Carroll

William Arens

ON THE FRONTIER OF CHANGE MTO WA MBU, TANZANIA

THE UNIVERSITY OF MICHIGAN PRESS
ANN ARBOR

LIBRARY

JUL 2 9 1981

UNIVERSITY OF THE PACIFIC

383414

Copyright © 1979
William Arens
All rights reserved

Published through the Imprint Series,
Monograph Publishing.
Produced and distributed by
University Microfilms International
Ann Arbor, Michigan 48106

Library of Congress Cataloging in Publication Data

Arens, W   1940-
   On the frontier of change Mto Wa Mbu, Tanzania.

   (Anthropology series) (Monograph publishing : Imprint
series)
   A revision of the author's thesis, University of Virginia,
1970.
   Bibliography: P.
   1. Mto Wa Mbu, Tanzania—History. 2. Mto Wa Mbu,
Tanzania—Social conditions. 3. Mto Wa Mbu, Tanzania—
Social life and customs. 4. Social change—Case studies.
I. Title. II. Series: Anthropology series (Ann Arbor, Mich.)

DT449.M7A73 1979   967.8   79-18843
ISBN 0-472-02714-X

CONTENTS

Maps   vii

Tables   ix

Preface   xi

I.   Introduction   1

     The Study of Social Change   4
     Planned Social Change   10

II. The Physical and Economic Setting   13

     Land and Agriculture   18
     Irrigation   22
     Fishing   26
     Marketing   27

III. Historical Development   31

     The Colonial Era   31
     The Post-Independence Era   39

IV. The Community and Its Residents   43

     Population Characteristics   43
     The Rangi   46

The Chagga   51
The Iraqw   58
Conclusion   60

V.   The Development of a Community Structure   63

     Internal Cohesion: Swahili Culture   64
     Internal Divisions   72
     Religion   78

VI.   The Politics of Unity   89

     Tanu   89
     Voluntary Associations   94

VII. Kinship, Marriage and Religious Adoption   99

     Kinship   100
     Marriage Patterns   108
     Ethnicity and Marriage in Urban Centers   114
     The Religious Process   119
     Case Studies   126

VIII. Tribalism and the Rural Center   137

     Rural Development   139

     References   143

MAPS

1. Tanzania, showing location of Mto wa Mbu   14

2. Mto wa Mbu and surrounding areas   15

3. Geographical origins of major ethnic groups
   in Mto wa Mbu   49

TABLES

1   Population by Locality   44
2   Age Distribution of Male Heads of Household   45
3   Ethnic Groups Represented by Permanent Residents   47
4   Selected Ethnic Groups: Percentage of Population
    1957-69   48
5   Heads of Household with Kinsmen and Affines
    in Residence   103
6   Heads of Household with/without Kinsmen and
    Affines in Residence by Year of Arrival   104
7   Percentage of Mixed-Ethnic Marriages
    by Time of Marriage   111
8   Percentage of Mixed-Ethnic Marriages Contracted after
    Arrival by Type of Marriage and Length of Residence
    when Married, and by Economic Interest in Traditional
    Homeland   112
9   Percentage of Mixed-Ethnic Marriages by Religion
    of Men and by Time of Arrival   113
10 Percentage of Mixed-Ethnic Marriages Contracted after
    Arrival by Religion of Men and Type of Marriage   114
11 Selected African Urban Communities: Mixed-Ethnic
    Marriages and Residential Stability   116

PREFACE

This monograph is a revised version of a Ph.D. dissertation submitted to the University of Virginia in 1970. More detailed comparative discussions of some topics have previously appeared in print and are cited in the text. I am grateful to the International African Institute for permission to reprint a portion of an article co-authored with Diana Antos Arens, originally published in *Africa*.

The major portion of the field research was conducted over a sixteen-month period during 1968-1969 as a Research Associate of the Department of Sociology, University of Dar es Salaam, supported by an NIMH Fellowship and Research Grant (PHS Grant No. 1T01MH11414-01). A return visit to the community in the summer of 1973 was made possibly by a State University of New York Research Foundation Grant-in-Aid. The support and cooperation of these agencies, as well as the aid of numerous Tanzanian officials, is gratefully acknowledged.

Information was gathered in a traditional manner by attempting to participate as fully as possible in the community's social life. In the process, I was graciously accepted and assisted by numerous residents who shared their experiences and memories with me. The research was conducted in *Kiswahili*. Formal training in the language prior to entering the field, and the patience of often amused friends, allowed me to dispense with a translator after a few months. In addition, a social survey of every tenth household

(N = 111) and a survey of male marriage patterns (N = 223) were carried out by myself and two assistants near the end of the field stay.

In addition to the formal debts, I have incurred a number of more personal ones. At the University in Dar es Salaam, my family and I were befriended and immeasurably helped by Paul Puritt, Emile Snyder, and Walter and Beverly Brown. In Arusha, we often enjoyed the hospitality and solace of Dr. and Mrs. Arjan Chopra and Mr. and Mrs. Ian Macauley. While in Mto wa Mbu, the tedium of daily living was regularly relieved by Iain Douglas-Hamilton, who was conducting research in neighboring Lake Manyara National Park. They were responsible for some of our most pleasant moments and fondest memories of Tanzania.

While a graduate student, I had the good fortune to meet Ivan Karp and Michael Kenny. Our relationship has always been instructive, and it has stood this test over the years. Upon coming to Stony Brook, I had the equally felicitous occasion to continue my education in anthropology at the hands of Paul Brown Glick and David Hicks, John W. Burton, Nancy Fairley, and Lawrence Taylor. The irrepressible Mari Walker, as the most indispensable member of the staff, has also earned my utmost gratitude. However, my major formal and personal obligations are owed to my teachers, William Watson, and E.H. Winter, who served as my dissertation advisor. My debt to them is more than I would care to admit and they would claim.

Finally, it remains only to thank and dedicate this monograph to Diana Antos Arens and Geoffrey W. Arens.

INTRODUCTION

Until recently the great majority of anthropological works dealing with Africa reported on the traditional structure of "tribal" groups. An important rationale supporting this approach was that the aboriginal social and cultural patterns of such groups would be radically affected by participation in an ever-widening social system. Paradoxically, the impression fostered by these studies was one of discrete socio-cultural units unchanging through time. It became apparent that this was only part of the total picture. Subsequently a number of monographs became available under the general heading of "social change" which focused on urban communities as a new aspect of social organization in Africa.

These two types of studies have resulted in a picture of Africa in which the rural hinterland is seen as remaining relatively static while the urban center is regarded as a scene of rapid social change. This is a mistaken impression. There are neither theoretical nor practical reasons to assume that change is taking place more rapidly at the urban than at the rural end of the continuum. Winter's (1955) study of economic and social change among the Amba of Uganda and Long's (1968) more recent one among the Lala of Zambia substantiate the assumption that both rural and urban communities respond to innovations which have an effect on traditional social patterns. This, of course, is neither a novel nor shocking suggestion. Nevertheless, it deserves to be stated since taken as a whole anthropological studies set in Africa seem to convey a different impression, even if unintentionally.

However, the sociological picture is still incomplete since in the African countryside other and possibly more profound changes are taking place with the emergence of new settlements reflecting characteristics of both urban and rural communities. For example, in 1920 Shorthose (1923) travelling through what was then Northern Tanganyika commented in a surprised manner on a little village describing it as:

> . . . inhabited by a polyglot crowd of natives who had emigrated from various inhospitable and barren districts, regardless of tribal distinctions, eventually to place themselves in this fertile little spot, under the guardianship of a Bahora Indian, by name Mohamed Ibrahim. Amongst other tribes, I found Wanyamwezi, Wenyiramba, Swahili, Warangi, Wafiume, Wambulu and Wambugwe (p. 250).

This monograph is concerned with such a community called Mto wa Mbu in contemporary Tanzania. It is similar to the village briefly described by Shorthose in that it came into existence in the early part of this century and its present population of 3,500 is composed of individuals from numerous ethnic groups who have settled in a new area which offers greater rewards for agricultural endeavor. This type of new rural settlement pattern is important from a social anthropological standpoint for various reasons. First, these communities are similar in a number of ways to urban ones: they are densely populated, composed of migrants, and culturally heterogeneous in character. At the same time, they are different in other ways since they are located in rural areas and have an agricultural rather than wage labor economic base. As a result, these communities do not fit into Southall's (1961a) dichotomy between the modern industrial and the traditional town or Epstein's (1967) distinction between the 'industrial' and 'civic center' as African settlement types. It is important, therefore, to determine what effects this rural ecological and economic character has on social patterns and processes which may be at variance from those found in urban areas.

Second, Mto wa Mbu exemplifies that not all migrants seek or prefer to settle in urban centers in order to improve their economic position, nor do those migrants who have previously lived and worked in the city necessarily return to agriculture in their original rural home. Both Watson (1958) and Van Velsen (1961) have convincingly argued that the rural migrant finds the city a place of basic economic insecurity, and that the great majority return home after a period of time. This description implies an uninterrupted movement between the city and the original rural home which, for Tanzania at least, ignores the fact that a small portion of these individuals move from one rural area to another and may never return home after their stay in urban centers. As a result, communities like Mto wa Mbu are constantly changing and growing while others of this character are being formed.

In the past indirect pressures encouraged the growth of these new types of settlements while the official policy of the colonial administration tended to restrict their development by ignoring them as best as they could. The district records (Masai District Book) make it apparent that to the European administrators poly-ethnic communites were felt go be somehow "untidy" and a source of inordinate problems in relation to their size. To use Bohannan's (1964) words, the colonial administrator's conception of Africa as an orderly "cupboard" with each item (tribe) in its proper place, was confounded by the mere existence of these communities. In Mto wa Mbu it was as if nothing was in its proper place. If a Nyamwezi or Chagga was not living in the confines of his traditional territory, he was being difficult.

Since independence some, if not the majority, of the African nations have emphasized rural-agricultural projects as opposed to the development of the urban-industrial sector of the economy. The Tanzanian government provides an outstanding example of a new nation attempting to implement this policy. To realize this goal Tanzania has actively encouraged in a number of direct ways the growth of communities such as Mto wa Mbu. These "villigiza-tion programs" as they are called are aimed at concentrating a scattered population into more densely settled communities in order to minimize administrative costs for various social services. As this study will show, this policy also provides an excellent opportunity for strengthening local-level political organization.

In East Africa these communities have been proliferating and becoming more important over time, but they have been almost ignored by social anthropologists. Abrahams' (1961) brief investi-gation of Kahama Township as a by-product of his study of the

Nyamwezi in Central Tanzania and Wazaki's (1966) and Ishige's (1969) articles on a similar village in Mbulu District of Tanzania remained the only works with an anthropological interest available on this topic for Africa until the publication of Vincent's (1971) monograph on local level politics in a rural poly-ethnic community. This study will seek to add to this limited body of knowledge, as well as to raise some broader questions concerning social trends in contemporary East Africa.

THE STUDY OF SOCIAL CHANGE

These brief comments on some of the salient characteristics of Mto wa Mbu suggest that the sociological analysis of the community falls primarily within the general scope of social change. Some discussion of the theoretical assumptions employed in the organization and interpretation of the data, therefore, is in order.

Social change is an extremely broad and general topic for the simple reason that change is an ever present feature of all social systems. There are no static societies, although for analytic purposes they have sometimes been treated as such. Firth (1964:56) argued quite succinctly that change is a dimension of the anthropologist's subject matter and not a separate division of it. As a result, in addition to being greatly misunderstood, discussions of change are often prone to vague generalizations about its nature, not to mention its causes. Much of this vagueness and confusion could be reduced by attempting to distinguish, at least initially, between different kinds of change and their various implications. From this level, it might then be possible to go on to broader discussions more profitably.

Firth (1959) was one of the earliest anthropologists to comment explicitly on types of change, discussing it in relation to his prior distinction between social structure and social organization. According to Firth, structural change involves readjustments "in the character of the social system" while organizational change involves some change in the way things are done in the particular social system (Firth 1959:340-342). Structural change, therefore, has more radical and profound consequences than the organizational variety.

This raises an obvious and important question. What, if any, is the relationship between the two? Although it is possible to distinguish theoretically between them, are they not aspects of the same social reality? Beattie (1961:170), in considering Firth's suggestions, has proposed that organizational change "inevitably entails at least some degree of structural change, as, for example, a decrease in the organizational importance of a lineage system, or of a chief-subject relationship, may, perhaps must, lead to qualitative (i.e. structural) modifications in the social system." Beattie does not conceive of the relationship between the two as being clear cut except in the realm of theory. Over time or through repetition organizational inevitably leads to structural change.

The ability to perceive of this relationship is a function of the availability of data over time. The longer the timespan for which there is reliable information, the greater the ability to perceive the manner in which minor changes ultimately alter the basic structure of a social system. Bearing this in mind, it was possible in this study through discussions with residents to follow the way the internal structure of Mto wa Mbu was shaped and reshaped over the few decades of its existence.

In some instances where the basic stimulus came from within the community, such as with the emergence of religious groups, the process was a gradual one. However, in another instance, the rapid growth of the local party organization almost immediately altered the structure of the community. The idea of political activity in support of independence was essentially an external one. This would suggest that the speed in which organizational shifts have on the existing structure is directly influenced by similar events which take place outside of the circumscribed social field in question. Nevertheless, in both cases it was the individual decisions by residents eventually had the effect of creating new structural configurations. The primary difference was the lapse in time prior to their being translated into more radical changes.

Mitchell (1966) also raises the question of the necessity of distinguishing categories of change with specific concern for clarifying some basic misconceptions surrounding the significance of urban communities in Africa. Mitchell allows that the behavioral patterns which have developed in African cities and towns are clearly different from those in traditional rural areas. This he feels has led many observers to label these phenomena too quickly as social change. He argues that this is an inaccurate description and one which can be clarified only by recognizing two distinct types of change. Mitchell suggests that "overall changes in the social system should be called 'historical' or 'processive' change, while the changes in behavior following participation in different social systems should be called 'situational' change" (1966:44). For example, the change in reckoning descent from the matri-lineal to the patrilineal line over a period of time would be an example of processive or historical change. However, the behavior of an individual in an urban community in which he recognizes kinship rights and obligations over a much wider range than in his traditional home is situational change. In this instance an individual's behavior has adapted in response to new social de-mands, but the rural social system of which he is a product has not altered because of this. If this distinction is not kept in mind and behavior in towns is interpreted against the background of rural social patterns, the misleading label of social change is applied.

Brokensha's (1966) study of Larteh in Ghana, Fraenkel's (1964) of Monrovia, and Epstein's (1958) on the then Northern Rhodesian Copperbelt are all typical studies of processive change since the analysis of data over an extended period of time is the common denominator. For example, in considering information over a twenty-five year span, Epstein (1958) was able to detail and interpret the circumstances which accounted for the change-over in a mine compound from a system of authority and repre-sentation by "tribal elders" to elected union officials. Other works, however, by investigating the individual migrant's adaption to the urban social system over a short period of time have em-phasized situational change as the main focus of attention (cf. Little 1965; Marris 1961; Mayer 1963; and Plotnicov 1967). Both types of studies usually involve implicitly a concern with the two kinds of change, but they tend to emphasize only one aspect. The confusion arises from the failure to distinguish explicitly be-tween the two. With these two different kinds of studies in mind I would like to return again to a consideration of Mitchell's essay.

As indicated, Mitchell's basic argument is that it would be misleading to infer processive from situational change. In Mitchell's frame of reference this means that urban behavioral patterns do not indicate subsequent changes of the same type in the traditional rural environment. Monographs based on field reports by Epstein (1958) and Watson (1958) among others, have validated this assumption.

However, Mitchell's discussion is based on a specific type of urban situation along the Copperbelt in Central Africa which is characterized by the steady circulation of migrants between the rural and urban areas. These temporal and spatial dimensions have influenced Mitchell's thinking to the extent of ignoring the relationship between situational and processive change when the urban social field is considered separately. As a result, it would be impossible on the basis of Mitchell's approach to account for those institutionalized behavioral patterns which have emerged in the city. What may be situational change vis-à-vis the traditional countryside is an aspect of what Firth (1959) has defined as organizational change within the urban social system. The specific types of situational adaption to the urban environment over time and the development of a settled population have an effect on the structural patterns of the city. This argument does not contradict Mitchell's basic assertion; rather it seeks to relate situational and processive change within the boundaries of the migrant community itself.

The approach to the study of Mto wa Mbu will seek to deal with the expression of the different forms of change. In addition to distinguishing between them, it will also show the relevance of the one to the other. The individual migrant's reactions to his new social environment in the form of the contraction of marriages, activation of kinship ties, the establishment of other relationships possibly based on religious conversion or political activity, in short, the development of social networks, will be dealt with as aspects of situational change. These were situational responses, however, which shaped and reshaped the structure of the community.

In describing the approach of this study, the term structure has been used often, and therefore it deserves comment. The decision to employ this concept raises basic questions about its usefulness in applying it to a settlement such as Mto wa Mbu, since it has so many characteristics of African cities.

Typical of others who have considered this problem, Mayer

(1963) and Epstein (1958) have pointed out in their studies of urban communities that in terms of "structure" there is a tremendous contrast between rural and urban areas. For the traditional rural social system, the concept of social structure has been the classical approach in social anthropology. It involves the explicit assumption that a tribal society can be understood through the study of the various institutions and their interrelationships which can be seen as forming an integrated whole. However, in cities an analogous structure is felt to be lacking by those who have carried out research. Mayer (1963) suggests:

> . . .the 'structure' which confronts us seems an immense tangle of criss-crossing interrelations involving many diverse and not logically co-ordinated roles and categories . . . we cannot see any overriding principles which articulate all these into a coherent whole. They remain on different planes; often one feels as if confronted by a social conglomeration rather than a 'structure' (p. 8).

The alternate approach in many studies of such communities has been to concentrate on social networks. The unit of analysis in this instance is a collection of individuals seen in relation to an ego as the central focus. Studies of urban areas or complex societies using this approach have yielded important results on the character of social relationships in this type of environment. The same approach will be utilized here to some extent as kinship, marriage and religion will be viewed as processual arenas within which an individual builds up a personal network for the purpose of accommodating himself to the social life of the village. The groups which emerge on this basis are ego centered and not permanent social entities. Religion, marriage, kinship and even ethnicity, therefore, will not be treated as structural features only but also as basic communal social processes. By doing so the focus of attention in this instance will be on situational change by describing the manner in which the residents adapt themselves to the demands of their new environment. This parallels the approach of the majority of urban studies.

At the same time though Mto wa Mbu is different from an urban community in many ways. The great majority of the migrants to the city arrive to find wage labor and after a period of time return home to the countryside. Their attitude toward the city is a negative one and they have no intention to settle there; instead as Watson (1958) has described it in discussing the Mambwe, they "raid the town" for short periods for economic gains. A basic factor to be considered then is the migrant's commitment to the city, which is weak in comparison to his attachment to his rural home. It is in the countryside among his kith and kin that he expects to return eventually; it is there that he intends to raise his children rather than in the city. Consequently, in the city few associations of permanence develop. Voluntary associations serve to meet specific needs and the composition of these groups changes rapidly or dissolves completely as the members return to the rural areas.

Mto wa Mbu, however, is a rural community of migrants and settlers who have not come to exploit it for short-term periods. The few who have come for this purpose, such as a number of traders, are a minority. The others have come to stay and to farm in an area far more fertile and with far fewer problems than their homeland. Consequently, although there is some variation, their commitment to the community as a new but permanent home is a strong one. For most there is neither the intention nor the desire to return from where they came. Their future lies in Mto wa Mbu.

This degree of permanence among the residents in a rural setting has resulted in the development of groups within the community which lend themselves to a social structural analysis. The significance of such an approach whether in the urban or rural setting, is that it aids in an understanding of social action. It is assumed that membership in permanent groups serves to generate some degree of regularity in the ordering of interpersonal relations. Within Mto wa Mbu, ethnic or religious identity, economic arrangements or participation in the political system has an effect on social behavior in much the same way as membership in a specific lineage, age grade or territorical section in traditional social systems.

Admittedly the collectivities found in Mto wa Mbu are not corporate and, therefore, often differ in this important manner from traditional ones. Futher, in some instances the social arrangements are imposed since they are the result of the community's integration with the wider social universe. They are, nonetheless,

sources of identity for the inhabitants and providers of values
as a guide to behavior. For this reason they will not be overlooked
entirely in favor of more ephemeral ego-centered networks. A
more complete comprehension of the social characteristics of the
village is gained by examining both processual and structural
aspects of organization.

PLANNED SOCIAL CHANGE

This brief discussion has attempted to put the study of Mto wa
Mbu into theoretical perspective, but there is another aspect of
this community which deserves comment and that is its relevance to contemporary developments in Tanzania. By emphasizing rural development Tanzania has placed tremendous
importance on change in the countryside and improvement in
the social and economic position of the inhabitants. Some of the
implications of this policy are: (1) a greater concentration of the
rural population into settlements as opposed to the typical East
African pattern of dispersed homesteads; (2) the encouragement of migration from one rural area to another for economic
opportunities rather than to the city only; and (3) as a by-product of these first two policies, the development of mixed-ethnic
communities where primary loyalty and identification is to the
community and thence the state. In short, the Tanzanian government is devoting a great deal of time, money and energy in order
to produce communities similar to Mto wa Mbu. Unfortunately,
it can not be said that they have been entirely successful in this
program. It is possible to state though that Mto wa Mbu is what
the Tanzanian government would like the countryside to be in its
ideal form. What is more interesting is that Mto wa Mbu developed
successfully into this ideal community during the colonial period
against the unofficial, but explicit, policy of the British administration. On the other hand, present attempts by the independent
regime to establish somewhat similar settlements through direct
aid and encouragement have not been as fruitful. It would be
interesting to consider some of the social developments and
resultant characteristics of Mto wa Mbu to determine why it has
become a model community for Tanzania.

This study was not conceived with this intention in mind, nor is any part of the body of this monograph, until the concluding chapter, again concerned directly with this problem. The topic is addressed because, during the course of fieldwork and in the process of becoming aware of the acute problems of development in Tanzania, it became increasingly apparent that such a concern would be relevant for consideration. As a consequence, it is hoped that this study will add to some small extent to the body of knowledge concerned with contemporary problems and goals of the Tanzanian people. If it does so, it may exemplify the manner in which anthropological research in Africa, which has fallen into such disregard of late, can reaffirm its concern for the Third World.

2

THE PHYSICAL AND ECONOMIC SETTING

The village of Mto wa Mbu is a little over seventy miles west by road from Arusha, the headquarters for the Arusha Region of Northern Tanzania. The community falls under the administrative jurisdiction of the Masai-Monduli District which is primarily populated by Masai and Arusha. Immediately to the west of the village lies Mbulu District, the home of the Southern Cushitic-speaking Iraqw.

The name Mto wa Mbu initially referred only to the village itself, but with the reorganization of the administrative system after independence Mto wa Mbu Division was created with the village as its headquarters. The Division includes a portion of western Masailand and a number of other smaller mixed-ethnic villages which lie on the main roads. In Kiswahili "Mto wa Mbu" means River of the Mosquitoes and is derived from the name of one of the streams which flows through the community. As the name suggests, the area is plagued by numerous malaria-carrying mosquitoes.

The village, originally defined as a minor settlement, lies at an altitude of 3,000 feet in the eastern branch of the Great Rift Valley and is situated at the base of the escarpment wall which rises 1,000 feet above the village. Three miles to the south from the center of town is Lake Manyara, which forms a link in the chain of lakes running through the Rift Valley.

Approaching Mto wa Mbu from the east heading toward the

14

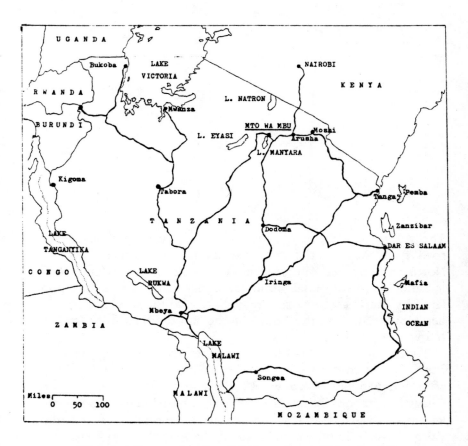

Map 1.   Tanzania, showing location of Mto wa Mbu

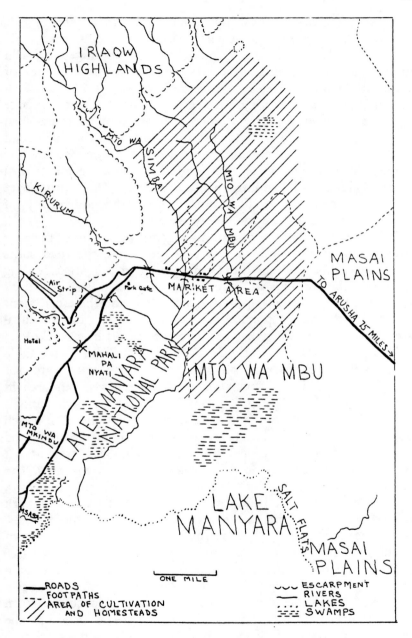

Map 2. Mto wa Mbu and surrounding areas

escarpment the dry plains of Masailand come to an abrupt halt with the emergence of a heavily wooded and cultivated area. The forest area which was formerly heavily populated by wild animals has been gradually cleared over the years. This area of cultivation marks the eastern boundary of Mto wa Mbu which then runs westward for almost three miles until it meets the base of the escarpment. The area under agriculture by residents then runs for two miles in a southward direction from the main road to the shores of the lake, while to the north it continues along the foot of the escarpment for approximatley five more miles until the plots gradually blend into uncultivated bush. The approximate amount of land under cultivation forming the community of Mto wa Mbu is about twenty-one square miles.

Farther along the main road is a game post, lower primary school, dispensary and local court. After a mile the road splits with one fork ascending the escarpment and the other leading directly to the entrance of Lake Manyara National Park. The park runs along in a narrow strip between the lake and the escarpment and the northernmost portion of the park borders on the cultivated area for a short distance before being cut off by the lake.

This segment is extremely fertile due to its high water table and proximity to a stream which serves as a source of water for irrigation, but it is a difficult and sometimes dangerous area in which to live and work. It is often frequented by park animals such as elephant, hippopotamus, buffalo and baboons all of which heavily damage crops while browsing or feeding in the cultivated fields. In addition to crop damage, the animals often attack residents in the area, especially at night and early morning. The park's proximity to this settled area of the village has been a constant source of conflict between the inhabitants and park management. While the residents are bothered by the animals, the management is in turn concerned about the small amount of poaching for skins and meat by the local people.

The center of the town is situated along the sides of the main road which runs through the village. The central area includes a number of cement buildings and a market place for produce grown in the area. The main crop is bananas which are purchased by the residents and travellers using the village road on their way to Arusha or Mbulu. Included in this area are four small retail shops selling sugar, tea, cloth and other small items; an African hotel and bar; and three other bars which sell both bottled and locally brewed beer.

Just to the rear of the market are forty-five cement houses built in 1968 by the Tanzanian government as part of its rural development program. The main reason for the construction was to present the many tourists who pass through the area and stop in the market on their way to the game parks with a favorable impression of rural Tanzania. Consequently, Mto wa Mbu in terms of housing is atypical of the Tanzanian countryside. However, the other houses off the main road where the great majority of the residents live are the usual wooden frame and mud type.

To the one side of the row of government built houses is the village's only "night club" owned by an enterprising Chagga woman. The "night club" is similar to all of the other bars in appearance. But, it has a special license which means that it does not have to abide by the standard opening and closing hours so that the normal business hours usually extend from 9:00 A.M. to midnight or later. Two rooms are devoted to the consumption of bottled beer and other liquors. Between the hours of 4:00 P.M. and 11:00 P.M. locally brewed beer which is made from either fermented bananas or sugar cane is sold in a separate room. Although the "night club" is frequented by the occasional resident, the main customers are the tour drivers who have left their passengers at the hotel on the edge of the escarpment and have returned to Mto wa Mbu for a night of drinking and possible dalliance with one of the girls who works there or in one of the other bars.

From the main road there are a number of small footpaths leading off to the fields (*shamba*, pl. *mashamba*) and houses of the inhabitants. The usual pattern is for each resident to build a house on his own land although in certain areas near the center of the village a number of houses might be built adjacent to each other. The village and the total area it comprises is unofficially subdivided by the inhabitants into various localities by names which describe some physical feature such as a stream or a prevalent type of vegetation. All the available land near the center of the village is under cultivation as well as the other choice spots immediately adjacent to the streams while the area between the streams is irrigated so that water is not a problem. The section to the east of the first stream bordering on the dry plains is gradually being cleared for cultivation as the population of the community expands. In addition to a lack of irrigation water this area also receives slightly less natural moisture since the rainfall is heaviest along the base of the escarpment at the western end of the village. However, at the present time the irrigation system is being extended to compensate for this problem.

LAND AND AGRICULTURE

Although Tanzania is relatively underpopulated in terms of the number of people per square mile, much of the available land is unsuitable for agriculture because of insufficient rainfall or for cattle keeping because of the existence of tsetse fly. It has been estimated (International Bank of Reconstruction and Development 1961) that only 30 to 40 percent of the country can rely upon sufficient rainfall for agricultural production. At the same time, these more favored and productive areas of the country are beginning to react to the pressures of overpopulation. For example, Gulliver (1969a) has reported that population density among the Arusha on the fertile slopes of Mount Meru had reached 2,000 per square mile in some spots by 1967. Similar conditions of enormous population growth have been reported by von Clemm (1965) for the Chagga on Kilimanjaro and by Winter and Molyneaux (1963) for the Iraqw highlands. The Iraqw have been fortunate in being able to expand into continguous areas with similar ecological conditions. The Arusha, Chagga and other East African agricultural peoples, however, have been less fortunate in that expansion has meant less favorable conditions for agriculture. Among these groups this has stimulated emigration from the original homeland into new areas in search of suitable land. Mto wa Mbu with its potentially fertile soil and abundant water provides an excellent opportunity for successful subsistence and cash farming.

In the early days of the community rights to a piece of land were established by residence. Any unclaimed, uncleared land was available to an immigrant by merely clearing the bush and planting crops. Consequently, the earliest settlers chose the best sites in terms of the availability of water. Consequently, their fields are usually the largest, as well as the most developed and productive. For example, one of the earliest settlers formerly had sixty acres under cultivation and produced a wide variety of fruit and vegetable crops which were marketed in surrounding settlements.

Since the area which comprises the community was not considered "tribal" land because it was not used by the Masai, rights to a piece of property were established during the colonial period by immigrants through requests to the District Headquarters via the government headman resident in the village. However, not everyone followed this procedure and clearing an unclaimed area was still the most common way of establishing rights to land. With independence the procedure became more formalized and now unused land can be obtained only through a request to the Village Development Council. The land in question is then examined by the Assistant Division Executive Officer and the Community Agricultural Officer for suitability and lack of prior claims. If the petition is granted, the owner receives the right to use the land on condition that the acreage is improved under his stewardship. Improvement in such a case would mean clearing, planting or building a residence. In theory, if this is not done, the land may be recovered by the state. When an individual requests a piece of undeveloped land which has been previously granted to another, the officers of the Village Development Committee may decide that the original owner has not fulfilled his obligations and reassign the parcel to the new petitioner. This usually leads to litigation in the local court.

Another means of securing land is through purchase. Although some land is still available for the asking, it is less desirable because it lies some distance from the furrows and, therefore, cannot be irrigated at the present time. Since the rainfall often proves to be insufficient, many of the recent migrants prefer to purchase a more desirable site from its present owner rather than accept potentially less fertile areas gratis.

Price varies with the quality of soil, the availability of water for irrigation and the distance to the market place. If the migrant is fortunate and has the cash there is still some opportunity to purchase excellent land. In most cases this occurs when the present owner has failed to clear some of his acreage and is willing to sell because of a need for immediate funds. The price in this instance for five uncleared acres would be between 400 shillings and 500 shillings[1] ($56. to $70.). The value would be increased if the land is cleared and at the time of purchase it is supporting crops. For example, an excellent farm of six acres with banana and other fruit trees and cleared land for maize was sold in 1967 for 1,400 shillings ($200.).

The amount of unoccupied farmland, even of second quality, is steadily diminishing. The expansion of the community is checked on all sides but one by the natural boundaries presented by Lake Manyara, the Masai Plains, and the Rift Valley Wall. Therefore, the days of rapid expansion and population growth due to immigration are coming to an end. The only possible area remaining for expansion lies to the north along the base of the escarpment and cultivation already extends for five miles in this direction from the main road. Distance from the road, lack of transport and roads means that further extension would be economically unfeasible at least for cash farming.

The basic crop cultivated by the residents is the banana of which there are several varieties. Some form part of the staple diet and are cooked whole in a stew with other vegetables or meat if it is available. Other types are grown for beer brewing or for eating uncooked. Maize is also cultivated and later ground into flour at the mill in the village for the preparation of a porridge type dish called *ugali*. Interspersed among the bananas and maize are other small plots devoted to vegetables such as cabbages, tomatoes, onions, peppers or beans. The established *shamba* usually also has a number of fruit trees bearing oranges, lemons, papayas or mangoes. In a larger *shamba* another area may be set aside for a cash crop of cotton or castor seeds. But since the typical *shamba* consists of two to four acres, cash cropping of this type is rare.

The reliance on bananas is due to the fact that it is used as part of the staple food while the surplus can easily be sold to the traders in the market. The importance of the banana is also enhanced by the relative ease of its cultivation since a single tree with enough moisture bears a single fruit stalk after only four months. Consequently, there is a steady supply throughout the year. While maturing a single tree will produce a number of other stems at its base. While the parent tree has yet to produce a fully developed stalk, the shoots at the bottom are removed. When the original stalk has almost matured, one of the young shoots is allowed to develop. Finally, when the parent stem has produced a stalk of bananas, it is cut down since it cannot bear again; the stem it has reproduced at its base continues to grow until it matures approximately three months later. This four-month cycle for bananas in Mto wa Mbu is a relatively short one due to irrigation and can only be matched in other areas of the country with a much higher average annual rainfall.

The banana is also more than a basic food crop, for it actually allows and facilitates the immigration process to the village. The natural process of growth which involves the reproduction of surplus offshoots which hinder the growth of the main plant means that these stems are available to others for the mere asking. Therefore, a new arrival can establish his own field at no expense to himself by requesting stalks from a neighbor, friend or kinsman already established in Mto wa Mbu. Finally, depending upon the location of his field he can have an available food supply within three to five months of arrival.

This basic crop, therefore, has implications which are of great significance beyond the arena of cultivation. In speaking with one of the oldest living members of the village and indicating my interest in its history, one of the first things he told me was of how in the early days when everyone had to rely on fish from the lake, one of the early settlers walked thirty miles through Masailand to Engaruka, another village of cultivators, and returned with the first banana plants. From these original stems the few inhabitants over time were able to begin growing the food stuff themselves. The passing of these plants from neighbor to neighbor was a means creating and cementing social ties through the process of giving and receiving. Each man received from someone the basis for a reliable and highly valued food supply and eventually passed it on to another. In a manner which is appreciated by the older residents the banana, as ordinary as it may seem, symbolizes the unity and mutual dependence of the community members.

Although many other events of the early days are obscured or entirely forgotten interestingly enough the history of the crops is vivid. I was told by many who brought the first papaya plants after a visit to the coast, while a second was remembered for introducing the first oranges and lemons. It is the banana, however, which is as significant in the present as it was in the past for it allows the village to persist and expand.

The cultivation of the two basic crops, bananas and recently maize, as well as the small quantities of various other vegetables and fruits, means an agriculturally self-sufficient household with a surplus available for sale in the market or in the case of cash crops such as cotton or castor beans to the village cooperative society. The average family can earn from thirty to fifty shillings per month depending on the size of the *shamba*. This income can then be used to purchase other household items such as coffee, tea, sugar, etc. and for the payment of the local taxes or the children's school fees.

Consequently the residents of Mto wa Mbu are in a relatively secure and advantageous position compared to inhabitants of other parts of Tanzania where the chances of producing enough food for household consumption can be a risky proposition because of frequent droughts. This is the most crucial factor accounting for the growth of the community through immigration and has resulted in a large increase in population over the last ten years.

IRRIGATION

The average annual rainfall for the four-year period from 1966 to 1969 was twenty-five inches with all but a small percentage falling in a single rainy season stretching from November to May. This twenty-five inch figure must be treated with caution since the rainfall in the area varies considerably from year to year. The records indicate that in 1967 and 1968 there were forty-four and forty-seven inches of rain respectively, but in 1966 only sixteen and in 1969 slightly less than fifteen inches. Watermeyer and Elliot (1943) set the yearly average at eighteen inches for the area which is a better representation of normal conditions. The extraordinary agricultural potentiality of this narrow belt is the result of the three permanent streams which run through the community, all of which originate in the highland areas of Mbulu District where the rainfall is much heavier. The streams run through the highlands then drop over the escarpment and flow through the village in a north to south direction emptying into

Lake Manyara. The fertility of the small area is further increased by a high water table and a number of underground springs which emerge at the base of the escarpment and crisscross the cultivated sections before joining with one of the streams.

In good years the rainfall is sufficient for the cultivation of maize and other vegetables, but the necessary minimal rainfall can not be relied upon and every few years the area experiences severe drought. For example, Lake Manyara after a normal rainy season is about twenty-eight miles long and ten wide at a depth of two to three feet, but has been reduced to isolated pockets of water by September in some dry years (Watermeyer and Elliot 1943 and Harris 1951). Although this is exceptional, less severe droughts are regular. Even under optimal conditions such as in 1967 and 1968 the rainfall was insufficient for cultivating bananas since they normally require about sixty inches of moisture per year to thrive successfully. This condition is usually only found on the cultivable higher areas of mountain slopes in East Africa. Hence, in Mto wa Mbu the high water table and the perennial streams for irrigation make banana cultivation possible.

The residents have irrigated since the area was settled by the early arrivals who cleared land near the streams and used irrigation ditches to reach their fields. As the community began to grow the rights to irrigation became more complicated, but they were still informal. In general, the older residents had the strongest claim to water usage on the basis of seniority and proximity to the source. The newer residents who were also using the same furrows would then decide among themselves the order of precedence, but this would also involve a recognition of seniority. Further, each subdivision of the village had a *jumbe* (headman) under the village's British appointed *jumbe* and any conflicts over water rights would be taken to the officer of the subdivision. However, there seems to have been little conflict over water rights in the past since there were so few residents in relation to the amount of water available. The existence of alternate water sources and the fact that during most of the year a number of irrigation ditches could tap the same stream mitigated against such conflict.

As the population began to expand rapidly in the early 1960s a greater degree of organization was required. During this period the responsiblity for control of the irrigation system was assumed by the local TANU (Tanganyika African National Union) branch through its village organization. Since Tanzania is a one party state and since the local TANU party chairman is the most important political functionary in the village, there continues to be little conflict. Each unit of ten houses forms a political cell with an elected leader who is also responsible for organizing the irrigation schedule in his area. The cell leaders of such an area meet together with one of their numbers whom they have chosen as the *mzee wa kijiji* (subdivision elder). Each of the six subdivisions of the community has such an officer and he has the authority to allot irrigation rights and to schedule usage. If more than one subdivision resorts to the same water supply, the subdivision party officers can work out an arrangement among themselves or take the matter to the party chairman for a decision. It is also the responsiblity of each cell leader to see that the irrigation ditches which pass through his area are kept in good repair through cooperative labor. In the event an individual irrigates without first securing permission he is fined ten shillings, but this has been a rare occurrence due less to the fine involved than to the desire to remain on cooperative terms with neighbors.

The degree of control exercised by the party over irrigation is illustrated in the following example. In 1968 because of heavy rains a number of families had to move since the lake had inundated their fields. Rather than return when the water subsided and risk flooding again, they decided to join together and form a *kijiji cha ujamaa* (socialist village) and cultivate collectively. The area they chose, however, was on the edge of the Masai plains and over a mile from the nearest water source. It was decided that another irrigation ditch leading to the new settlement would be constructed, under the aegis of the TANU organization, with the party chairman taking a personal interest in the project. The actual labor was divided up among the residents living in the areas where the canal would pass and the members of the new settlement.

The emergence of TANU as the arbiter of the irrigation system was inevitable during the years after independence. Its organizational framework encompasses the entire community while its officials have the legitimacy to regulate usage and forestall potential conflict.

One of the most signfiicant social implications of irrigation is

that its effective exploitation requires a large degree of cooperation among those relying on it for cultivation. In some historical
instances involving state organization and intensive usage such
cooperation has been insured by the exercise of control over
irrigation by centralized despotic authority (Wittfogel 1957).
Gray (1963), however, has reported that among the uncentralized
Sonjo of Northern Tanzania who have an irrigation based agricultural system, water rights are controlled by the elders representing various segments of the village. In this instance decisions
regarding its use are arrived at informally.

In Mto wa Mbu, as described, no strict regulation of water rights
was established on the basis of a formal authority structure but
cooperation among the settlers was maintained. Because of irrigation it was necessary for the inhabitants to generate cooperative
relationships. Each cultivator was forced to recognize that cooperation with his neighbors was essential to his own benefit.
This meant other considerations, for example that one's neighbor
was from a different ethnic group or had a different religion, were
submerged in view of the crucial fact that their economic security
depended upon the same source.

Irrigation, therefore, was more than the framework for cultivation; it was also a basis for social relationships, and insured that they
were maintained peacefully for the benefit of all. This does not
mean that conflict among the inhabitants did not exist; it did.
Rights to plots of unused land seemed to be common cause for
disputes. However, disagreements did not spread to the extent of
impairing mutual cooperation over this vital issue. Further, if any
one individual did not respect the rights and needs of others by
using the irigation ditches when and where he pleased, then the
entire community coalesced over this issue and restored con-
formity regardless of divisions over other matters.

To recapitulate, the reliance on an irrigation system necessitated first the establishment of social relationships among neighbors which in turn extended through the community since each
was dependent upon the other. Second, especially in the early
days of the community when formal agencies of social control
were lacking, irrigation provided a framework and opportunity
for peaceful social interaction on the grounds of mutual dependence. Ethnicity or religion were not relevant considerations. As a

result, relationships among the inhabitants were structured largely around the irrigation system. As the community grew larger and the problems grew more complex, control over the water system was inevitably assumed by the party, the most important organization in the community.

FISHING

The existence of Lake Manyara with its abundance of fish only three miles from the main road has been an additional attraction to migrants from parts of Tanzania where fishing has been a traditional pursuit. The main advantage of fishing is that it can bring in a constant supply of money on a daily basis while farming requires a waiting period until the crops have been harvested before a profit can be realized. However, only about twenty-five men in the village fish full time because of the prior skill involved and the danger of the hippopotamus which occasionally attack boatmen in the shallow water near the shore.

The fishing is carried out by one or two men using nets in a small boat. A good day's catch might include fifty tilapia and five to ten lungfish. The tilapia usually sell in the market place at five for a shilling and the lungfish at two for a shilling or more depending on size. Consequently, on such a day a fisherman can realize somewhere between twelve to fifteen shillings, assuming that all can be disposed of in the market place, where they are sold both fresh and smoked by the wives of the fishermen.

The majority of the fish caught are bought and consumed in the community, but a portion are sold to middlemen and transported to Arusha and other towns in the vicinity where a greater profit can be made. However, this is not done on any regular basis by the residents. Occasionally a resident will buy fifty or one hundred pounds of fish and transport it to Arusha by bus, but this is done rarely because of the risk of spoilage.

As would be expected, the greatest number of fishermen come from areas where it has been a traditional pursuit. This would include those from the Nyasa area of Lake Malawi and would account for the Nyanja in residence and some of the Sukuma of Tanzania from the area adjacent to Lake Victoria. Others from non-lake areas have also taken to fishing, but they are few because of the skills needed and the dangers involved.

MARKETING

The market is located in the center of the village and operates seven days a week as the focal point of activity during the morning hours. The site was formerly the building and storage area for a government housing project and is a vast improvement over the original location, since most of the traders' stalls are now under a tin roof which was used to protect the building materials.

Immediately to the front and outside of the enclosed area are a number of open-air shops which stock cloth, pots, pans and dry goods and a tailor's shop which is also occupied by the two shoe repairmen of the village. To the rear of the market are four small butcher shops which sell freshly cut beef and goats' meat. To one side of the market adding to the congestion and color of the scene sit the Masai women with their donkeys. The women have come from the surrounding plains to sell their milk to the residents and later return home with the small items they have purchased in the market and with water collected from a stream. The majority of the stalls in the market are devoted to the sale of fruits and vegetables while a few others sell only fresh and smoked fish. The area for fruit and vegetables is occupied by men. Only women sell fish since for a good part of the market day the men spend their time on the lake.

An annual license to sell in the market costs one hundred shillings and a local commercial tax of thirty-five shillings per annum is added. There is also a yearly local tax of forty-five shillings which must be paid promptly by the traders if they wish to remain in good standing. The total annual investment for a trader including his personal tax is 180 shillings which is a considerable sum for the average resident. The other alternative is to pay a half shilling per day which covers both the license and tax; this arrangement is the most common since few men have the 135 shillings available at the beginning of the year.

In most cases where a stall is operated under an annual license two men will be trading with one man paying the owner of the license a weekly or monthly fee. If this arrangement works out satisfactorily the following year they will share the cost of a new permit. In most instances the two men are either kinsmen or members of the same ethnic group since they feel that this insures the necessary cooperation and trust involved. This can be contrasted to the conceived unimportance of ethnicity among the cultivators. For the traders the ideology of a common cultural background is employed to cement the bond between partners (Arens 1973).

The market contains only thirty-six stalls and one half of these are occupied by members of one ethnic group, the Chagga, who are all Christians. The other traders represent a number of different groups, and are a mixture of Christians and Muslims with the latter predominating. Marketing on a comparatively large scale is undertaken only by some of the Chagga who buy bananas in large quantities from the local farms and then make arrangements to transport them to nearby towns and cities. The other traders are content to deal in smaller quantities and to restrict their sales to other residents or the odd traveller.

Some of the traders also have a small *shamba* and they sell their produce from it and other purchased items at their stalls. The larger traders deal mainly in items they have purchased for resale in the market. The few traders who deal in large quantities can average a profit of 400 shillings to 500 shillings per month, while the small scale operators might average between fifty shillings and 100 shillings.

Since almost everyone in Mto wa Mbu owns a *shamba*, a great portion of the produce, especially the bananas, is purchased by non-residents and consumed outside the community. Regular trips are made by traders from other areas for the purpose of buying bananas and transporting them by bus or truck. For example, one entrepreneur arrives twice a month with a large truck which he fills with banana stalks, sometimes as many as one hundred, and transports them to Dodoma over 250 miles away for resale. A venture of this sort can net the trader a profit of close to 1,000 shillings per trip.

However, the greater portion of the crop is purchased by travellers and drivers who pass through the market. Since the community is located on a main road connecting it to a number of other cities and settlements, the traffic is considerable. Rarely will a traveller pass by without stopping to purchase bananas because of the reasonable price. Usually the driver for a private firm, or even the driver for a government agency will stop on the way to his destination and fill up his available space with bananas in order to resell them personally for a small but quick profit. Although this is a rather irregular form of commerce, the volume of traffic insures that it brings in a regular and sizable income to the community.

NOTE

1. One East African shilling is equivalent to fourteen cents.

3

HISTORICAL DEVELOPMENT

Except for some of the areas of West Africa, both the large and small towns of tropical Africa are the result of outside non-African stimulus whether of European or Arab origin (Steel 1961). Mto wa Mbu is no exception to this rule; but it is not the result of a direct external influence provided by the establishment of a European administrative post or Arab trading center. It is instead the by-product of various changes which took place in the settlement pattern of East Africa during the early years of the colonial administration. As a consequence, the character of Mto wa Mbu's historical development can be seen as a reflection of these external forces emanating from the imposition of colonial rule. More recent changes have taken place in the community as a consequence of other trends and new policies which have been inaugurated since self-government was achieved.

THE COLONIAL ERA

The area which now encompasses the settlement of Mto wa Mbu was in the early twentieth century an uninhabited forest belt in the western portion of Masailand. Archaeological evidence, however, does indicate the existence of settled agricultural villages of unknown groups prior to the arrival of the Masai throughout this portion of the Rift Valley (Sassoon 1967). For obvious reasons the area has always had an attraction for cultivators. During the immediate pre-colonial era the plains immediately to the east of the forest and the highlands above it were controlled by the Masai. The latter territory above the valley, although thinly inhabited by Masai, was given a wide berth by the Iraqw to the south and was not settled by them until the establishment of European rule. The Mbugwe living just to the south of the forest in the lowlands also left the area unsettled as a buffer between themselves and the Masai.

The Masai themselves avoided the forest area for a number of reasons, the most important being the numerous tsetse flies which posed a threat to their cattle. Further, although the area was well watered, the Masai as non-agriculturalists had no interest in clearing land for cultivation. The large concentration of wild game and malaria-carrying mosquitoes further detracted from the advantages of the area for pastoralists. Consequently, this potentially fertile strip of land running along the base of the escarpment remained uninhabited from the early seventeenth century until the 1920s.

The colonial administration had a profound effect on this pattern. Areas within the large expanse of Masailand which were unused but suitable for cultivation were encroached upon by other ethnic groups in the colony such as the Chagga, Arusha, Meru, and Pare who lived on the slopes overlooking the plains (Southall 1961b). Thse fertile highlands were experiencing population increases, and in some places, for example the Pare hills, soil erosion was becoming an increasing problem (Kimambo 1969). Fortunately for these groups, the presence of the British provided the necessary protection for subsequent population movements. As a result, some of the territorial arrangements in East Africa, in particular those adjoining Masailand, experienced a degree of fluidity unmatched in the immediate pre-colonial era.

The realignment was not only the result of the British colonial presence, for the Arabs and for a short period the Germans were also the agents of change. The trade settlements established on the coast and along inland caravan routes of East Africa by the Arabs stimulated certain groups in the interior such as the Nyamwezi, Yao and Kamba to undertake their own trading expeditions from the hinterland to the coast (Roberts 1968). The Nyamwezi of Central Tanzania were exceptional in this regard and in addition to their own trading endeavors they served as guides and porters for other caravans as well as for the first Europeans who penetrated East Africa. By 1912 they were already recorded along various centers on the coast of Tanzania and Kenya (Southall 1961a).

The arrival of the Germans along the Tanzanian coast in the late nineteenth century and their attempts to establish their rule in the interior also involved a degree of physical mobility, mainly for certain few coastal individuals in the service of the colonial administration. The Germans, as compared to the British who worked to a greater extent with indigenous political structures and personalities, relied to a larger extent on members of the coastal groups as their agents in other areas (Trimingham 1962). After some degree of training and education under the Germans these individuals were sent to the interior as soldiers, policemen, tax collectors and overseers of European agricultural projects. Coupled wth the harshness of German rule this proved to be a disastrous policy culminating in the Maji-Maji uprising against the Germans and their agents in 1905. At the same time, the system provided many of the African functionaries with experience outside of their own territory. With these experienced travellers Mto wa Mbu had its start in the early years of British rule in Tanganyika.

It is difficult to precisely pinpoint the founding of the village. The change from an uninhabited forest to a small settlement of a few cleared fields was a gradual one. Various groups in the community see the emergence of Mto wa Mbu in terms of the arrival of their predecessors. Before that it is assumed that there were just isolated individuals. As with the histories of ethnic groups, dynasties or even nations, people with vested interests see the past events in terms of their own position in the present and interpret events accordingly. Consequently, some of the oldest Muslim residents from the coast state that Mto wa Mbu had its start with the settlement of coastal peoples. The implication is that there was no community in the sense of a group of related individuals until the establishment of Islam. On the other hand, the Nyamwezi and Sukuma in residence say that the village had its origins with the arrival of a small group of their own predecessors after World War I.

These various interpretations of the past are more important in a sociological than historical sense since they are an indication of contemporary internal divisions within the community. During the period of fieldwork there were still residents in the village who were among the earliest settlers, and, therefore, it was possible to establish with a fair degree of accuracy the founding of the community.

In 1917 as part of the World War I East African campaign, German forces composed of Europeans and a few hundred African porters and *askari* (soldiers) left the Musoma Region of Northern Tanganyika and headed southeast. After passing through the Serengeti Plains and the highlands of what is now Mbulu District, they descended the escarpment into the Rift Valley. They camped near the former iron-age site of Engaruka which although in the heart of Masailand was already under cultivation by non-Masai including Nyamwezi, Sukuma and some coastal peoples. The little village also served as a trading station. Their next day's march brought them thirty miles further south where they camped at an existing caravan site (Watermeyer and Elliot 1943) on the edge of the forest which was later to become Mto wa Mbu. At that time there were no inhabitants in the area except for the Masai in the plains, but it seems that the possibilities of the site were apparent to some of the African members of the expedition.

One of the German members of this force, still living and farming a few miles away in Mbulu District, returned to this encampment site in 1927 and found a small number of people farming. A number of the original settlers were Nyamwezi and Sukuma who had been with the 1917 German force. This would correspond with the belief of the Nyamwezi living in Mto wa Mbu that some of the first inhabitants were other Nyamwezi who had served with the Germans during the East African campaigns of World War I. According to this version, a number of these former *askari* who were at the time living in the administrative site of Arusha received the permission and encouragement of the colonial officials to clear the uninhabited area for cultivation. Whether or not there were already a few people in residence is a matter of dispute by the older inhabitants. As indicated, in 1917 there was already a non-Masai agricultural settlement thirty miles to the north and it is possible that a number of these people also shifted south to Mto wa Mbu. In any event, assuming the former *askari* to be the first residents, the founding of the village can be placed sometime in the early 1920s.

The population remained small and stable until the early 1930s when a road from Arusha to the European settlement of Oldeani thirty miles to the west passed through Mto wa Mbu and climbed the escarpment just to the west of the village. This new road attracted a few Indian traders to Mto wa Mbu who acted as middle men in transporting fruits and vegetables grown in Mto wa Mbu to the European settlements of Arusha and Oldeani where the Europeans had concentrated their resources on growing coffee and wheat for the world market. This also meant that the inhabitants of Mto wa Mbu had an outlet for their crops for which they received cash. The new road and the possibility of cash farming attracted many more immigrants. However, at this time many new arrivals came only to exploit this factor and did not remain as permanent settlers. The idea was to farm for one or two years growing and selling bananas, oranges, tomatoes and onions which were in great demand in the European communities and then return home with the money. The farm was then left vacant and would be taken up by another who would do the same for a few years. These individuals, however, were only a small portion of the residents, and undoubtedly, many who intended to stay for only a short period of time remained indefinitely. In doing so, a permanent settlement was established and continued to grow, slowly drawing in numbers from individuals representing various Tanzanian ethnic groups. This movement in and out of the village by a small portion of the residents is still a characteristic feature of Mto wa Mbu.

The community is first mentioned in the District Book for Masailand in 1935. It was recorded at the time that on Jubilee Day, 1935, a contingent of *Waswahili* (Swahili people) from Mto wa Mbu arrived at the District Headquarters in Monduli for the ceremony and: "Their dance, well executed, formed an interesting contrast to those of the Masai." It was also recorded at the time that Mto wa Mbu with a taxpaying population of approximately 300 was designated as an "alien" (non-Masai) agricultural settlement within Masai District. Further, it was decided that because of the amount of potentially fertile land available and the lack of interest by the Masai in the area, the number of immigrants would not be restricted. Therefore, permits from the District Office to open new plots for cultivation would not be required.

However, the growth of other similar alien settlements in Masailand were strictly controlled because of the limited land resources available. In order to implement this policy, it was necessary for intended migrants to these settlements to receive permission from the District Office. This lack of administrative control over the admission of new residents to Mto wa Mbu meant that in addition to the average migrant, any individual who had run afoul of the traditional or colonial administration in his own district could move into Mto wa Mbu and melt into the population without presenting himself to the government authorities. This was probably a fairly common occurrence and resulted in giving the village the reputation of being inhabited by tax dodgers, thieves and other assorted undesirables. Other factors discussed below also contributed to the unsavory reputation of the community.

During this period the village was administered by a British appointed *jumbe* (headman) who in turn appointed headmen for the various localities. Their duties included tax collecting, law enforcement, and hearing minor cases under the jurisdiction of a native court which was established in 1938. The legitimacy of their position was seriously undermined by the lack of any traditional supports so drunkenness, fighting and petty theft were reported to have been common. This, of course, added support to the idea that the village was heavily populated by deviant characters, an idea which survives to an extent to the present. I was told by a party official from district headquarters that "many things which do not meet the eye take place in the village." This impression along with the numerous drinking places and congenial barmaids working in them has given the community somewhat of a sinister reputation among outsiders. At the same time, it has a certain fascination for them since in many ways the community has a number of similarities to frontier towns of the American West. The residents on their part deny all of this and consider themselves to be honest industrious farmers.

By the early 1950s Mto wa Mbu had a population of about 1,200 as compared to the 1967 figure of almost 3,500. A survey of the ethnic origin of the migrants in relation to year of arrival indicates some fairly definite trends. As mentioned, the Sukuma and Nyamwezi, along with some of the coastal peoples such as the Zigua, Nguu and Segeju, were among the earliest inhabitants. The survey indicated that the majority of them had taken up residence between 1930 and 1950 although others of the same ethnic background continue to filter in up to the present. These people are representative of those individuals who were caught up in the changes of the colonial era and moved throughout Tanganyika as soldiers, porters, laborers and low-level administrators before deciding to abandon their traditional homes and settle in Mto wa Mbu.

The second distinctive wave of migration took place in the late forties and early fifties and consisted in large part of individuals from the Central and Northern Tanzanian areas. These included representatives from the nearby Mbugwe, as well as others from the further off Rangi, Iramba and Gogo. The main attraction of Mto wa Mbu for these individuals was the ease and security of farming there as compared to that in their original homeland where cultivation was more precarious.

During this period members of various other ethnic groups took up residence in the community, but the earlier settlers lent a certain character to the community. These groups were all overwhelmingly Muslim, and, consequently, they succeeded in establishing Islam as the dominant religion. They were also successful in converting many other immigrants from their traditional religion to Islam. This coupled with the fact that their primary interest was in agriculture gave form to the community.

In the 1960s the village experienced a third wave which while greatly expanding the population also had qualitative effects. This most recent stage witnessed the arrival of a large number of Chagga and Pare from Northern Tanzania who are overwhelmingly Christian. A portion of these new arrivals came not only to farm, but to trade, open shops and engage in skilled labor such as tailoring, carpentry and shoe making. As a result, during this period there was an enlargement of the market, the initiation of larger scale trade and the building of retail shops, lodgings and bars owned by Africans which challenged the trading monopoly of the Asian shopkeepers. This period also saw the establishment of a Lutheran, Seventh Day Adventist and Catholic Mission which competed with the existing Mosque. Consequently, the character of Mto wa Mbu was transformed from that of a small Muslim agricultural settlement to a busy developing mixed religious as well as poly-ethnic market community taking advantage of a heavily travelled road.

This outline of the development of Mto wa Mbu up to the early 1960s clearly reflects the strong relationship between the growth and changes in the community and other forces which were operating at the national level. It can be appreciated, therefore, that Mto wa Mbu in its formative period was a product of the opportunities and changes initiated during the colonial period.

First, the majority of the earliest residents were those individuals who were direct participants in the colonial system as part of the governmental administration, soldiers or wage laborers. Second, communities such as Mto wa Mbu with its mixture of migrants from various ethnic groups arriving as individual settlers in an alien area were unknown in East Africa except for the coast until the colonial period. Such a phenomenon was due in large part to the widening of physical and social fieds made possible by the colonial presence. It is not being proposed here though that until the imposition of colonial rule the interior of East Africa was characterized by a static population. Information provided by recent anthropological and historical research has corrected this false impression.

Studies have also illustrated the significance and regularity of internal population movements as well as the process of assimilation of individual migrants from one ethnic group into another (Cohen and Middleton 1970). The situation reflected in Mto wa Mbu was different since the residents were not assimilated into the structure of the surrounding groups nor did they wish to be. Further, the village was not incorporated as a unit of the Masai political structure. Rather it was administered directly from the colonial District Headquarters through a resident political functionary since the legitimacy and security of this new settlement were based on its relationship to the colonial rather than to the indigenous social system.

Just as trends in the early colonial era were reflected in the characteristics of the first settlers, the later migrants to Mto wa Mbu represented the changes emerging in Tanzania in the years immediately preceding and following independence. These later arrivals came predominantly from some of the more fertile areas of Tanzania such as the slopes of Mounts Kilimanjaro and Meru and the Pare Hills. In this case the stimulus for emigrating was due to the pressures of overpopulation. In addition, these new migrants were from a different social background as compared to that of the established residents. They were, as mentioned, generally Christians and relatively more educated and progressive. Also, their interests and what they hoped to achieve for themselves and their families in Mto wa Mbu were somewhat different than that of their precursors in the community. Other new settlers of this type undoubtedly believed that with independence economic opportunities would become more accessible to the African population and consequently sought their fortunes in settlements where trade had been a traditional monopoly of the resident Asian shopkeepers. Whatever the motivation, the emergence of a significant African trading population in Mto wa Mbu dates to the early years of self-government. This factor along with other changes which took place as a result of Tanzanian independence had a profound effect on the organizational character of Mto wa Mbu.

THE POST-INDEPENDENCE ERA

Although the colonial system might have been largely responsible for creating conditions favorable to the founding of Mto wa Mbu, the official attitude toward the village could best be described as uninterested. For example, the total amount of information available on Mto wa Mbu during the era of British rule consisted of two brief mentions in the District Book and a small file largely concerned with matters pertaining to the years just prior to independence. During this period the administration's attention was directed toward the Masai. This was quite natural since the overwhelming majority of the residents of the district were Masai and their problems should have assumed paramount importance. As a logical consequence administrative services and projects were geared toward meeting the needs of the Masai inhabitants. This not only reflected a practical approach to government, but also a philosophical orientation on the part of the colonialists which stressed the value of the continuity of indigenous societies. This was compounded by the positive attitude of many European officials toward the Masai whom they considered a proud, independent people unwilling to change their traditional ways. Paradoxically, other groups more responsive to changes and showing an inclination toward "westernization" were less admired and also presented greater administrative problems. The colonial government was concerned with improvements in the Territory, but such policies were aimed at producing changes without intentionally upsetting the mode of life of the peoples involved or affecting relationships between various groups. In discussing the subject of British rule in East Africa, Gulliver has stated that "the net effect of the colonial era was a marked heightening of tribal consciousness and a deepening of tribal differences" (1969b:16).

Mto wa Mbu provides a striking contrast to this situation since it was established during the colonial era and had a population which sought to de-emphasize ethnicity. As an anomalous farming community within an immense area populated by cattle-keeping people, it was all but overlooked during the British administration of the District. Also, since it was populated by migrants from other areas and, therefore, lacked a traditional political structure, it had to be dealt with in a different manner than the other parts of the District. Along with the lack of a traditional system of authority, the mixture of residents meant that a single body of customary law could not be applied in the community and this further compounded the confusion and aura of untidiness which surrounded the settlement. During the entire period no development projects were initiated, few services were provided to the residents and official visits by administrators were infrequent. The same conditions prevailed for all other such "alien" agricultural settlements in Masailand.

With the coming of independence in 1961 the situation was altered radically. The departure of the British and the installation of an African administration was accompanied by a discernible shift in attention by this new regime away from the countryside to more densely populated rural settlements like Mto wa Mbu. For Masai District this meant that the numerous pastoralists scattered throughout the area were no longer of greater significance than the inhabitants of the agricultural settlements which had emerged during the years of British rule.

This shift in orientation and values was the result of a number of factors stemming generally from policy decisions formulated at the national level by the new government. First, the decision was made by the Tanzanian government to encourage rural rather than urban industrial development. Since the overwhelming majority of the rural residents are small scale cultivators this meant an emphasis on agricultural development. Secondly, this program of rural development involved an attempt to provide greater social services to the inhabitants of the countryside than they had previously experienced under the British. This meant encouraging more compact rural settlements and increasing the importance of those already in existence as centers for these services. For economic and administrative purposes it was decided that these central locations could more efficiently serve the needs of the inhabitants of the village and surrounding countryside. Mto wa Mbu was a natural site for the implementation of this policy since it exhibited all of the necessary characteristics for this purpose. Thirdly, a reorganization of the governmental structure involving the creation of smaller administrative units below the district level resulted in the creation of Mto wa Mbu Division with the community as headquarters for a large area including a portion of the outlying Masai plains. In effect, this meant that part of the traditional Masai country fell under the jurisdiction of Mto wa Mbu while previously the opposite had been the case.

In addition to these explicit policy formulations, other factors underlie the increased importance of these communities. The replacement of British by African officials also meant a change in attitude toward the Masai. The typical African administrator does not see the Masai and other conservative groups as proud members of noble "tribes," but rather as backward, and as a category lacking the proper consciousness necessary for contributing to the growth of a modern progressive nation. Hence, the new administration has subjected the Masai to programs encouraging them to wear trousers and shirts in place of their traditional cloaks and to stop piercing their ears and other practices which are considered barbaric by many other citizens. Finally, the fact that these new communities have been important outposts in the rural areas during the independence movement and in the present day give firm support to the party, has not been lost on the government. For example, while the Masai and other such groups in the vicinity such as the Iraqw and Wambugwe took little interest in these matters, the residents of Mto wa Mbu organized the first local branch of TANU in the District from whence it was spread to other small settlements. The response of the government has been to involve these centers of strength in the machinery of rural development and administration.

For Mto wa Mbu this has meant the establishment of a local court with two trained magistrates and a police post, the opening of a dispensary with a small hospital and a soon to be expanded primary school. The increased importance of the community was also reflected by an influx of government employees and the stationing of various officials whose primary duties were related to the developmental needs of Mto wa Mbu. The presence of these individuals in addition to the school staff, medical personnel, court officials and policemen along with the nearby employees of the National Park has also produced a group of residents who are dependent on the goods of the local economy. Finally, in response to the needs of these bureaucrats and in recognition of the numerous tourists who pass through the area, the government sponsored the building of forty-five housing units and brought piped water to the village.

This can be contrasted to the situation which existed during the colonial period when the inhabitants of Mto wa Mbu were left to their own devices. The community has always, even during the era of British rule, reflected what was new and changing in the country; however, under the European administration, it was ignored in favor of what was traditional and stable. With independence this growing village not only represented what was new, but also what was desired, and, therefore, it was given government support. Mto wa Mbu reflects the new Tanzania while the surrounding countryside represents the old. This is also understood and appreciated by the residents of the community who consider themselves to be forward looking and in many ways primarily *wananchi* (citizens) of a new country as compared to the closeby Masai and Iraqw who are seen as relics of the colonial past.

4

THE COMMUNITY AND ITS RESIDENTS

The migrant character of the community is revealed by information compiled from the 1967 Tanzanian Census which indicated that only slightly less than 10 percent of the adult inhabitants of the two detailed sample areas were born in the community. Mention has already been made of the fact that the overwhelming majority of the present residents have migrated to the village from various other parts of Tanzania. A small percentage although born outside of the country had previously established residence in Tanzania and came to Mto wa Mbu from cities or European plantations where they had been engaged in wage labor.

This chapter will be concerned with providing some basic demographic and sociological characteristics of the population relative to the pattern of immigration. In addition, a more detailed analysis of the representatives of three specific groups in the community will be undertaken. Although migration to Mto wa Mbu may have taken place on an individual or family basis, these studies will illustrate that members of the same ethnic group have adjusted to the community in a particular manner.

POPULATION CHARACTERISTICS

In 1967 the division for which Mto wa Mbu serves as administrative headquarters contained a population of 13,094. Enumeration areas within the village itself indicated that there were 3,414 residents at the time of the census. The remaining 9,600 people included Masai who were incorporated in the Division, but lived outside of the village in the surrounding hinterland.

For census purposes the Mto wa Mbu settlement was broken down into eight areas reflecting recognized geographical localities. An examination of these figures (table 1) indicated that the sex ratio favors males over females among the residents which parallels the situation found in most African cities and towns. Such an imbalance is understandable in larger industrial or administrative urban centers where the typical migrant is an unmarried male or married man who has left his wife and family behind in the rural area while working in the city. This pattern is feasible since he normally returns home after a short period to rejoin his family.

The proportion of males to females in an agricultural community such as Mto wa Mbu, however, should reflect a more equal

Table 1. Population by Locality

Locality	Males	Females	Total	Households
Mbugani	291	260	551	180
Mbugani Chini	66	67	133	42
Migungani	165	114	279	103
Majengo	212	153	365	99
Manyara	414	282	696	169
Jangwani	285	199	484	145
Barabara Juu	239	205	444	102
Migombani Juu	245	217	462	109
Total	1917	1497	3414	949

Source: Tanzanian Census 1967, Enumeration Areas. (Raw data supplied by Tanzanian Census Office, Dar es Salaam, Tanzania).

sex ratio since it is a relatively settled population and the work unit of agricultural production is normally a division of labor among the family members. The reason for this disproportionate ratio is due to the fact that not everyone living in the community is a cultivator. For example, the Manyara locality which has the highest imbalance includes the area encompassing the Park and Game Department Headquarters and the employees of these two organizations are all males who have come to the community for wage labor. In doing so they reflect a pattern similar to what is found in the city where men leave their wives and families at home.

A similar argument, however, would not hold for the other localities which are agricultural. A partial answer to this question is provided by the number of young men who have come to Mto wa Mbu as traders, farm laborers and government officers. But, more important is the common procedure for the agricultural migrant to the village to arrive by himself. Only after having bought or cleared a piece of land and built a dwelling place will he have the rest of his family join him. For these reasons at any one point in time, therefore, there will be more males than females.

The figures on age distribution (table 2) conform to what would be expected in a rural community. In contrast, the urban centers

Table 2. Age Distribution of Male Heads of Household

Age	Number	Percent
Under 20	4	2.4
20-29	34	20.6
30-39	41	25.0
40-49	43	26.0
50-59	17	10.3
60 and Over	26	15.7
Total	165	100.0%

Source: Tanzanian Census 1967, Enumeration Areas.
(Raw data supplied by Tanzanian Census Office, Dar es Salaam, Tanzania).

usually show a predominance of men under forty-five years of age; those over this age are forced back into the countryside because of the lack of agencies of economic support for those who can no longer find work. The older migrants who retire permanently to the countryside are in turn replaced by younger men moving the other way and taking their place in the city. As a result, a constant labor supply composed of young migrants is maintained in residence (Epstein 1958). The figures for Mto wa Mbu indicate that although it is composed of migrants, the older residents remain in the community rather than return home.

Information on the ethnic origin of the inhabitants on a systematic basis was only available from 1957 onwards (Masai District Records). The following list (table 3) includes the ethnic affiliation of male heads of household who were engaged in agriculture or trading as permanent residents of the community, but it does not include information on individuals posted to the community as government officials.

This listing gives no indication of the relative strength of ethnic representation in Mto wa Mbu. Table 4 (see page 48) provides these data over a twelve-year span and also illustrate the percentage increase and decrease of selected groups during this period.

Table 4 shows that since 1957 the largest ethnic groups in the village accounted for between 67 percent and 74 percent of the population and the remaining 26 percent to 33 percent was spread out among over fifty other groups represented in Mto wa Mbu. For at least the last two decades, therefore, no single ethnic group in the community has been able to achieve a position of dominance based on numerical superiority. The figures also illustrate the relative increase of decrease in strength of some groups over the twelve-year period. Briefly, the Chagga, and to a lesser extent the Pare, have shown substantial increases while the proportional representation of the Sukuma and Nguu have decreased during this period. The Rangi, however, have remained the largest ethnic bloc throughout the twelve years.

THE RANGI

The Rangi have been chosen for discussion because for a considerable period of time they have been one of the major ethnic groups in the community and by 1969 they were the largest. The Rangi migrants in many ways also typify a particular process of adjustment to the community which is characteristic of other settlers and, therefore, they serve as a model for assessing the relationship

Table 3. Ethnic Groups Represented by Permanent Residents[1]

Ankole (Uganda)	Kisii (Kenya)	Rangi
Arusha	Kuria	Rongo
Bena	Lambia	Ruanda
Burungi	Luguru	Rufiji
Chagga	Luo	Rundi (Burundi)[2]
Digo	Makonde	Safwa
Fipa	Makua	Sambaa
Ganda (Uganda)	Mbugwe	Sandawe
Gogo	Mbunga	Sangu
Gorowa	Meru	Segeju
Ha	Mwera	Shashi
Haya	Nandi (Kenya)	Sukuma
Hehe	Ndali	Sumbwa
Ikizu	Ngoni	Taita (Kenya)
Ikoma	Nguu	Taveta (Kenya)
Iramba	Nyakusa	Turu
Iraqw	Nyika	Wanga (Kenya)
Isanzu	Nyamwezi	Wasi
Jita	Nyanja (Malawi)	Yao
Kamba (Kenya)	Nyasa	Zanaki
Kerewe	Pare	Zaramo
Kinga	Pimbwe	Zigua
Kipsigis (Kenya)	Pogoro	

[1] The decision to define a group as a "Tanzanian tribe" is based on Gulliver (1959). Consequently, certain groups, particularly the Luo, Digo, Makonde and Nyasa, are included even though the major area of their land lies outside of Tanzania immediately across a national border.

[2] Representatives of the Bantu agricultural class of traditional Burundi society. Commonly referred to as Hutu.

of ethnic identity to community organization.

The Rangi are classified by Murdock (1959) as members of the Rift Cluster of the Tanganyika Bantu which also includes the Gogo, Iramba, Wambugwe and Turu. Along with the Rangi these latter four groups have provided numerous migrants to Mto wa Mbu. The Rangi themselves number over 100,000 in their original homeland which lies approximately one hundred miles due south of Mto wa Mbu (map 3). Their traditional diet includes a prefer-

Table 4. Selected Ethnic Groups: Percentage of Tanzanian Population, 1957-69

Tribe	1957	1967	1969
Chagga	1.7%	11.0%	12.6%
Iramba	8.5	8.0	5.0
Iraqw	1.5	9.5	.9
Nguu	5.1	.5	.9
Nyamwezi	3.8	7.6	3.6
Pare	.9	7.0	5.0
Rangi	14.9	7.6	16.0
Sukuma	17.0	4.7	6.0
Turu	6.0	7.0	5.0
Wambugwe	7.9	5.0	8.0
Zigua	*	6.6	2.7
Total	67.3%	74.5%	65.7%

* Not available.

ence for cereal crops and in Mto wa Mbu they are exceptional in their emphasis on the cultivation of maize rather than the ever-present banana. Traditionally they also are a cattle-keeping people, but they, like all other residents, keep no stock in Mto wa Mbu because of the tsetse fly. In the event that a Rangi does own cattle which he may have inherited he keeps them at his original home in the care of a kinsman.

A glance at the location of the Rangi on the ethnographic map of Tanzania indicates an interesting feature. Although Bantu people, the Rangi have no common boundary with other Bantu speaking groups. To the west and east they are bound by the Para-Nilotic Masai and Tatog while to the north and south by the Cushitic Iraqw, Gorowa and Burungi. Further, compared to both their Bantu and non-Bantu neighbors the Rangi claim a greater number of adherents to Islam. This was the consequence of an Arab trade route which started on the coast at Bagamoyo and passed through their territory in the late nineteenth century on its way to the interior commerical center of Ujiji on Lake Tanganyika. Some of the older Rangi residents of Mto wa Mbu have added that the small village of Kondoa in the center of Rangi

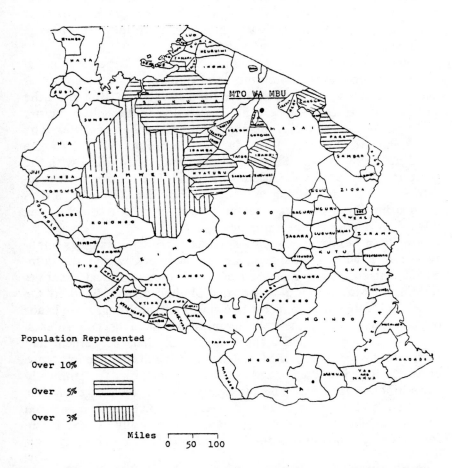

Map 3. Geographical origins of major ethnic groups in Mto wa Mbu

country which straddled the route was also part of an inland trading network which included Engaruka, the village thirty miles north of Mto wa Mbu. It is very likely then that some Rangi were already represented in the area as traders in the early part of this century and through their wanderings were familiar with the virgin area which became Mto wa Mbu.

Compared to the Chagga who have the second largest numerical representation in the community, the Rangi provide a number of marked contrasts. First, they have been in Mto wa Mbu from the earliest days since 44.4 percent had settled in the village before 1950 while another 27.7 percent immigrated before 1960. The remaining arrived after 1960 during the period which saw the rapid influx of Chagga. Second, all the Rangi are Muslims with the great majority professing Islam on arrival. The remaining few accepted it after establishing residence in the village. As with settlers from other areas they have taken little interest in trade choosing instead cultivation as their primary concern.

Finally, an extremely significant fact is that the Rangi exemplify a group with a wide-scale kinship network within the community itself. Sixty-one percent had consanguineal relatives residing in Mto wa Mbu at the time of their arrival. Further, the survey indicated that in 1969 two-thirds of the Rangi male heads of household had close consanguineal kinsmen as co-residents. Another 17 percent had affines, while less than 20 percent had neither consanguineal nor affinal ties in the village. The existence of a large Rangi isolate has provided the opportunity for ethnically endogamous marriages. The males have taken advantage of this, since only 11 percent of their marriages involved a woman from another ethnic group. This compares dramatically to the figure for mixed ethnic unions (40 percent) for the community as a whole.

Although the Rangi form a large segment of the population, they in no way stand out as a distinct community group. Compared to the Chagga, they are not heavily involved in the commercial affairs. Along with the majority of the other residents, the Rangi have resettled to farm because of the precarious nature of agriculture in their own district. Further, as Muslims they are a submerged integral part of the most important religious association in the village.

As long-term residents, they have created a network of relationships crossing ethnic boundaries. Although the males show an inclination to marry another member of their group, numerous Rangi females raised in Mto wa Mbu have married men from other ethnic groups in the village. Finally, the existence of a larger number of kin in proximity has meant that some of an individual's most important relationships and personal events are contained by the social boundaries of the community. In short, the Rangi blend into the community so that their presence is significant only in reference to numerical strength.

THE CHAGGA

The Chagga have been mentioned often in the preceding pages in a number of contexts. Their arrival in large numbers during the 1960s had a profound qualitative as well as quantitative effect on the community structure. In many important ways they have failed to blend into the social life of the village as it existed upon their arrival, but instead have manipulated and altered it to suit their own interests. Most significant is the fact that they see themselves as forming a distinct entity in Mto wa Mbu and this distinctiveness is in turn recognized by others. A brief examination of social change among the Chagga in their homeland during the colonial era will provide a historical background for a consideration of their adaption as migrants to Mto wa Mbu.

Although situated approximately 150 miles from the East African coast, their homeland on Mount Kilimanjaro has been in contact with foreign influences for centuries. During the mid-eighteenth century one of the various Arab trade routes to the interior passed through their territory and a trading station was established. Although the Chagga did not develop their own trade routes to the coast, they traded heavily with passing caravans in ivory and reportedly to some degree in slaves (Low 1963).

By the later part of the same century after a short period of resistance, the Chagga were forced to submit to German rule. The most important by-product of the short period of German administration was the limited acceptance of coffee as a cash crop but it was not until after World War I and under the British Mandate that coffee cultivation emerged on a large scale.

The cool climate, abundance of water, traditional irrigation system and good soil provided optimal conditions for coffee. Since it can be cultivated among the banana groves which provided the staple food supply, their subsistence economy was not disturbed at the time the crop was introduced. Consequently, the Chagga eagerly accepted this innovation and by 1924 a cooperative society was formed for the production and marketing of the coffee (Ingham 1965). During this period schools and missions were opened in large numbers and European education was readily accepted. By the 1920s the Chagga had a higher standard of living than was common at the time and in general devoted themselves to their cash crop as a source of income rather than seeking wage employment outside of their homeland. Unfortunately for the Chagga this situation could not last forever since the higher standard of living produced a natural population increase which resulted in tremendous pressure on the land. According to one estimate, by 1945 there were already 600 people per square mile in Chaggaland (Bates 1965) and in 1957 it had climbed to 950 (von Clemm 1964).

The slopes of Kilimanjaro which were under cultivation before the arrival of the Europeans are characterized by a series of ridges and valleys. In the pre-colonial era a single ridge was occupied by a clan which maintained its own system of irrigation by damming a stream and constructing furrows leading off to all areas of the ridge (Pike 1964). Possibly because of this type of irrigation system conflict among clans was prevalent and warfare among them endemic. During the colonial period the system became more complex with single water sources serving a number of different ridges.

The original and most intensively cultivated area is a highland belt between 3,500 and 5,000 feet above sea level where rainfall and streams were sufficient for the cultivation of the banana which was and remains the staple food. In addition to being their basic food, the banana was used for the brewing of beer while the plant provided thatching for their huts as well as fodder for cattle. The lower slopes of the mountain were avoided because of the lack of rain, the absence of irrigation furrows and fear of the Masai on the plains (Brewin 1964).

At the present time, the system of land tenure is characterized by dual holdings, one field under ideal conditions is situated in the high fertile belt while another is located in the drier lowlands. Although it is not stated explicitly in the available sources (Brewin 1964; Johnson 1946; and Pike 1964) it is likely that the prevailing system developed during the colonial period which permitted Chagga exploitation of the lowland areas in close proximity to the Masai. Nevertheless, if possible, the cattle are still left in the highlands to remove the temptation for raids.

The field located in the highland area is called *kihamba* (pl. *vihamba*). The *kihamba*, situated as it is in the uplands, is the traditional and most valuable holding where a man will build his house and cultivate the two most important crops, coffee and the banana, in order to provide food and a cash income. The *kihamba* can be bought, sold or inherited and has been described as the "freehold" land of the Chagga (Brewin 1964).

Under ideal conditions the cultivator will in addition to his *kihamba* have another plot located in the lowlands called *shamba* (pl. *mashamba*). On this field supplementary cash and food crops such as cotton and maize are grown and if possible some grass which is cut and dried before being brought up the mountain for the cattle. This land can not be sold or inherited, but is used with the permission of the local authority and at the death of the holder reverts backs.

As an indication of the extent of population growth it was reported in 1945 that the average size of a newly granted *kihamba*, i.e. a plot given to landless Chagga, was about 100 square yards. This can be compared to three-acre grants of twenty years earlier. As a result, by that time the better *mashamba* fields were already being converted into *vihamba* holdings as the scarcity of the former increased (Johnson 1946).

The system of inheritance through the fragmentation of holdings further increased the pressure on the land. Traditionally and theoretically the father's *kihamba* was inherited by the youngest son who remained home with his parents until their death while his elder brothers were settled on other fields (Johnson 1946). However, as *kihamba* land steadily diminished a family head was forced to divide his field among his sons. The result in many cases was a *kihamba* plot too small in size to support a single growing family. This accounts for the number of Chagga in Mto wa Mbu who reported that they still retained a small field at home which they hoped to return to in their old age.

The situation among the Chagga in the 1950s could be summarized as follows. They were highly educated, progressive and enjoyed a higher standard of living than the average Tanzanian. At the same time, population pressures necessitated some degree of emigration. Although some moved into the cities where they found a place in the colonial social system, many others began to spread out through rural Tanzania in search of suitable agricultural land and other economic opportunities such as to be found in Mto wa Mbu.

The tremendous and rapid influx of Chagga into the community can be understood clearly from an examination of the population figures on ethnic affiliation (table 4). A colonial survey (Masai District Records) of Mto wa Mbu in 1957 reported that only 1.7 percent or 8 out of 469 households were occupied by Chagga. However, by the 1967 census 11 percent of the population of the community were Chagga and a survey of the inhabitants carried out in 1969 during the course of fieldwork indicated another 1.6 percent gain increasing the figure to 12.6 percent. The survey also indicated that 85.7 percent had arrived in Mto wa Mbu since 1960 while the remaining few arrived over a twenty-year period between 1930 and 1950.

In addition to the fact that they are recent arrivals, the Chagga in Mto wa Mbu exhibit a number of other differences. First, although the community is predominantly Muslim (64.0 percent) the Chagga inhabitants are overwhelmingly Christian (85.7 percent). The arrival of the Chagga, therefore, has had a tremendous impact on the religious make-up of the community. If the Chagga were discounted, the Christian population of Mto wa Mbu would be reduced from one-third to less than one-quarter.

Secondly, the Chagga exhibit a degree of "clannishness" uncommon in the community. For example, only 10 percent of the Chagga men have ever married non-Chagga women while the figure for inter-ethnic marriages in the community is four times as large. This is related to the fact that the majority of the Chagga males have married before emigrating. Nevertheless, the few young Chagga on whom information is available had all returned home to marry, and others indicated they would only marry a Chagga female, preferably one from their own district.

A survey of language usage pointed out that in 21 percent of the Chagga households only the traditional language is used, while the comparable figure for the entire community is 10 percent. In addition, in one-half of the Chagga households the traditional language was described as the principal one, while the other half employed *Kiswahili*. This is undoubtedly related to the previously-mentioned fact that fewer inter-ethnic marriages were contracted by Chagga. Consequently, it is possible to rely on the traditional idiom as a means of communication in the household. As a result, the children become fluent in their own language, while for others *Kiswahili* is of greater importance. This is worth noting, since von Clemm (1964) has reported that among the Chagga in their own homeland, the traditional language is rapidly being replaced by *Kiswahili*, the official language of Tanzania. This is not supported by observations from Mto wa Mbu since the Chagga language is frequently heard, even in public, while individuals from other ethnic groups normally speak *Kiswahili* together. If von Clemm is correct in his assumption, then the Chagga language will survive longer in poly-ethnic communities where it has the function of maintaining cultural identity.

The majority of the Chagga as well as the other migrants to Mto wa Mbu came to cultivate; however, another segment arrived primarily to engage in small-scale retail trade which may or may not also include some farming. For example, in addition to the previously mentioned fact that eighteen of the thirty-six stalls in the market are run by Chagga, all four of the African shops are owned by Chagga; three of the four butcher stalls are Chagga owned; all three bars selling bottled beer and European liquor are the property of Chagga; and two of the four bars selling local beer are owned by Chagga. Added to this, 50 percent of the skilled craftsmen, e.g. tailors, shoe repairmen, carpenters and masons, are Chagga.

Consequently, when the three Indian shopkeeping families are excluded, trade in the village is primarily in the hands of this single ethnic group. This factor of economic dominance rather than the cultural characteristics of the Chagga which set them off from the other residents of the village. Their arrival has also meant a growth in trade as well as the physical expansion of the community. It has not meant jobs for other residents though since normally the Chagga hire co-ethnics to work for them. The usual procedure is for the proprietor to bring one of his own kinsmen or a friend from his home area to work for him.

Considering all of these factors, the Chagga represent a specific way of orientating to the community. For the traders, Mto wa Mbu is merely a place to conduct business and in no way does it represent a true home. For some of them Mto wa Mbu is just one of the places where they have an investment and they may spend almost as much time out of the village as in it. Further, if they consider economic opportunities more promising elsewhere they have no hesitation in moving. As one trader in the market said: "I plan to spend two or three years here collecting enough money to move to Musoma to open a small retail shop. If that goes well, I would like to return home to marry and open another shop in my village." The interest of these individuals in Mto wa Mbu is almost entirely economic. Their other interests lie outside of the village where their family and kinsmen continue to live in their traditional home. The social orientation of the Chagga in Mto wa Mbu in many ways parallels that of the majority of African urban migrants whose interest in the city is short term and primarily economic.

Those Chagga who have come primarily for agriculture also exhibit a number of other peculiarities. In the area containing the best farmland because of the abundance of water for irrigation, it was found that one-quarter of the heads of household were Chagga. Considering that they compose only 12.6 percent of the total population, a greater portion of them than would be expected on a random basis are situated on some of the best land. Since all of this land was occupied before their arrival in the early sixties, this meant that they were able to purchase farms. This can be contrasted to the normal procedure where the typical migrant requests uncleared, unclaimed land through the Village Development Council. This land is granted free with the intention that it be cleared for agricultural production. The Chagga by comparison have had the funds on arrival to purchase cleared well-watered and productive fields.

Another interesting and indicative characteristic feature of the Chagga in Mto wa Mbu is uncovered from an examination of their

kinship ties in the community. Only 21.4 percent of those surveyed had consanguineal kin and/or affines living in Mto wa Mbu
when they arrived, and during the survey period in 1969 only
42.8 percent had either type of relative in the village. Considering
the community as a whole for comparison, it was found that
one-half of the population had some form of kin or affine in
residence when they arrived and two-thirds had some sort of
relative in the village by 1969.

Because of these social and economic characteristics, other
inhabitants recognize the Chagga as a distinct group in their midst.
The Chagga are seen as occupying an advantageous economic
position because although they are relative newcomers, they have
managed, nevertheless, to secure some of the best land and within
a short period of time to have come to dominate local trade. Also,
from the viewpoint of the Muslim majority in the community,
the Chagga form the backbone of the emerging Christian population. They have seriously affected the state of religious homo-
geneity based on Islam which existed prior to their arrival. Finally,
the failure of the Chagga to establish affinal ties through inter-
ethnic marriages within the village has added to their social isolation. Thus they lack the cross-cutting ties, at least those based on
marriage and kinship, which would serve to unite them to other
groups in the village. As a result, to define someone as a Chagga
implies something definite about the individual's social niche in
the community.

It must be emphasized, however, that their distinctiveness is
not based on peculiar cultural characteristics. Ethnic groups in
this sense are not relevant to the structure of the community. The
Chagga are singled out as a recognizable social entity because of
their occupational interests and more importantly because of
their dominant position in the economic structure. Mitchell
(1970) has pointed out that in Africa ethnicity and class often
coincide in poly-ethnic centers. The situation of the Chagga in
Mto wa Mbu substantiates this observation. The Chagga are best
seen as an emerging class with ethnic identity serving as the sym-
bol of their economic position (cf. Arens 1973).

It is possible to argue, therefore, that the Chagga illustrate
the process of "retribalization" as described by Cohen (1969:2)
in his study of Hausa minorities in Nigerian urban centers. He

describes the process as the formation of new political groupings along ethnic lines in the struggle for economic and political power.

This regrouping of the Chagga in the pursuit of new goals, however, has not been translated into political competition. Also, this "clannishness" is not openly commented on by other residents. The ideology of the state and the community as well which continually stresses the unimportance of ethnicity prevents discussion of the Chagga as a isolated group within the village. For the same reason the Chagga themselves do not unify for political purposes. Ethnic politics are clearly incompatible with the prevailing ideology but the same can not be said within the arena of economic competition.

THE IRAQW

The Iraqw have been singled out for comment since as a group they also illustrate another particular kind of social adaption to the community. The proximity of their traditional territory has provided the Iraqw in Mto wa Mbu with options not available to other villagers who have come from a greater distance. This spatial dimension has affected the character of their social relationship to the community as a new home and source of personal identity.

Living in the highlands just above the community are the Southern Cushitic speaking Iraqw. Compared to the Masai who live three miles to the east of the escarpment wall on the other boundary of the cultivated area the Iraqw exemplify a slightly different type of accommodation to the village.

The Iraqw are traditionally both agricultural and cattle-keeping people and their land in most places is ideally suited for both. The streams which run through Mto wa Mbu originate in this area due to the heavy annual rains in the highlands. In the past, the center and density of the Iraqw settlement was much further south of Mto wa Mbu than it is today (Winter and Molyneaux (1963). In the late nineteenth and early twentieth centuries the area above the escarpment to the west of Mto wa Mbu was left unsettled by the Iraqw as a buffer zone between themselves and the cattle-raiding Masai who were to the north of them. However, in the twentieth century as a response to population pressures and with the colonial administration as an artificial buffer between them and the Masai, the Iraqw began to expand northward until they reached the area immediately above Mto wa Mbu. This closer proximity to the Masai, even during the present, however, is hazardous since the Masai continue occasionally to raid the Iraqw for cattle.

The Iraqw representation in the community (table 4) indicates a peculiar trend over the years. In 1957 they were listed as forming 1.5 percent of the population and in 1967 the government census listed them as 9.5 percent of the heads of households. However, information collected in 1969 showed only 0.9 percent of the heads of households in the community to be Iraqw. This sudden population fluctuation in only two years was probably due to the heavy rains and flood of 1968 which forced many of the Iraqw to abandon their fields in Mto wa Mbu and return to their original homes in the highlands just a few miles away.

The return to their original homeland during the floods is important as an indication of their relationship to Mto wa Mbu. The great majority who were living in the village came from an area just a few miles away where they continued to retain rights to land. In that area they kept their cattle and in most cases devoted their acreage to growing wheat for cash, while in Mto wa Mbu the shamba was used to grow bananas, maize and other vegetables for domestic consumption. The Iraqw in Mto wa Mbu, therefore, maintained what could be described as a dual residence.

Since they had not settled in the community because of adverse conditions in their own district, they immediately returned to the Iraqw highlands while the other residents were forced to remain in Mto wa Mbu trying to seek shelter. The commitment of the Iraqw to the community as a "home" is non-existent or at best a weak one. Their interest is in terms of exploiting its agricultural potential for economic benefit. Their main social interests and important relationships are outside of the community in their nearby homeland.

Other individuals who reside in Mto wa Mbu might well be described in this manner to a lesser extent. The Iraqw, however, provide the perfect example of a group with this exploitive presence in the community matched possibly only by the Chagga's involvement in commercial enterprises. For the Iraqw this is possible because of their own rich land where they have retained an economic interest in the form of cattle and fields. Consequently, they are less dependent on their investment in Mto wa Mbu.

Further, the proximity of their close kinsmen provides for a continued preoccupation with developments at home. As a result many of their interests are channelled outside of Mto wa Mbu which contrast with those individuals who have left their homes and travelled some distance to secure better land and a higher standard of living in Mto wa Mbu. The greater distance from their kinsmen and friends whom they have left behind also acts as a stimulant in drawing them into the affairs of the community. In short, these individuals in comparison to the Iraqw can be described as true residents of the community. To a much greater degree their future lies in the social and economic contacts they have established in Mto wa Mbu and in the continued development of the community. The Iraqw on the other hand have remained what the other residents refer to as *watu wa kabila* (tribesmen).

CONCLUSION

This chapter has examined the way in which settlers from different traditional ethnic groups have adapted to the community. The Rangi, Iraqw and Chagga were selected because each illustrates a specific process. The Rangi typify a mode of absorption into the social and cultural life of the village which is characteristic of the great majority of the residents by de-emphasizing common ethnic identity in the establishment of relationships with co-residents.

For different reasons the other two groups discussed chose an alternate course which has involved the retention of ethnic identity and traditional relationships. The Iraqw have opted in this manner because of the proximity of their homeland and the resulting ability and interest in maintaining a dual residence. The Chagga, both cultivators and traders, have utilized common ethnicity in order to maximize their control over the economic rewards available to residents. As a result of their diverse social and economic interests neither of these two groups have committed themselves entirely to Mto wa Mbu as a permanent home.

However, these individuals are a small segment of the population with unique interests in the community. The majority of the residents believe that regardless of origin they are in the most important ways a single people and prefer to use the terms *Waswahili* or *wananchi* to refer to themselves. They take pride in the fact that "tribalism" is not an obvious feature of village social life. The recognition of common needs and values and the realities of social patterns which cross ethnic boundaries underlies this conception of their community.

When questioned specifically about the possibility of the existence of different types of residents and the basis for classification, many will admit to the existence of such divisions. Ethnic identity plays some part in the construction of these categories, but not the most important, and then only in conjunction with other considerations. The characteristics of these groups and their relevance is the concern of the following chapter.

5

THE DEVELOPMENT OF A COMMUNITY STRUCTURE

The remarks of the introductory chapter suggested that structural models had received relatively little attention in the earliest studies of urban African communities. The failure of traditionally defined corporate groups to make their appearance intact in the city seemed to be the basic reason for the abandonment of this classic anthropological approach in the initial monographs. Some time later, subsequent works revived the structural model with their emphasis on urban ethnicity as a primary facet of urban social organization. It became apparent to students of this milieu that, in the struggle for scarce economic and political rewards in the city, common ethnicity emerged as a basic organizational principle. However, as the previous chapter indicated, it was not possible to generate such a model for Mto wa Mbu, since in most contexts ethnic distinctiveness was deemphasized in favor of a common community-wide identity. The rural agricultural character of the village and the irrigation base rendered such considerations irrelevant to the residents, if not counter-productive.

Nevertheless, it is possible to discuss basic organizational principles in Mto wa Mbu which are at variance with urban social patterns. However, having drawn attention to the model, it is not suggested that all the relevant social behavior of the residents will be comprehensible. There are other considerations including active participation in groups outside Mto wa Mbu having an effect on behavior. Also, within the community itself individuals are presented with great opportunities to manipulate situations and choose among alternatives in the ordering of social relationships, the most important of these being the possibility of joining an existing group.

This flexibility is made possible by divisions within the community based on cultural identity, religious persuasion or participation in the local political organization. The manner in which individuals choose from among these options and the various social patterns which finally emerge as a result can be more fully appreciated.

The following pages, therefore, will be concerned with the role religion, cultural groups and finally the local political organization play in dividing and joining the community along various lines. The social processes which stimulated the emergence of these groups will receive as much attention as the character of the groups themselves.

The first step in such an effort is to determine if and on what basis the residents of the community see themselves as forming a distinguishable social-cultural category with regard to the outside world. Specifically, is there a well-developed sense of internal solidarity, and if so, is this unity recognized by outsiders?

INTERNAL COHESION: SWAHILI CULTURE

A major factor contributing to a sense of distinctiveness of the inhabitants results from the physical location of the village and the relationship of the community to the traditional groups of the surrounding countryside. Most of the migrants did not come from the immediate area, but usually from some distance (map 3). The bordering Masai have not contributed to the village with settlers because of their disdain for agriculture and preference for cattle keeping. The other two closest groups, the Iraqw and Wambugwe, also keep cattle in addition to cultivating and as a result took little interest until recently in settling in the village. Also, as described earlier, for the Iraqw residence is usually only on a part-time basis. This can be compared to Abrahams' (1961) description of the mixed-ethnic town of Kahama in the center of Nyamwezi country in Tanzania. In his survey of the composition of the town he found that nearly half of the inhabitants were

Nyamwezi which was an indication of the close relationship between Kahama and the surrounding countryside. He also points out that the township was administered until independence as part of an encompassing Nyamwezi chiefdom. In effect, it was part of a larger unit and integrated with it in a number of important ways. As a result, Abrahams felt that Kahama was not fully developed either socially or politically as a distinct community within Nyamwezi country.

Mto wa Mbu by contrast has been defined from its inception as a distinct socio-political entity in Masailand both by the administration and by its residents. The fact that the migrants came from afar meant that there was from the beginning a sharp break in the spatial dimension of social relationships between the village and the countryside. This lack of important interpersonal ties extending from within the community to the surrounding population has had the effect of socially isolating the residents of Mto wa Mbu from the immediate area. The inhabitants of the village do, of course, interact with the Masai, but these relationships are best seen as being between members of different communities.

In general, the relationship between Mto wa Mbu and its hinterland is similar to that found in any other part of the world as a reciprocal bond between the permanent center and the more scattered population. Mto wa Mbu with its market place and shops gives the Masai an opportunity both to buy and to sell items. Each day the Masai women come into the village with gourds of cow's milk which they sell to the residents of Mto wa Mbu at the market place. For the right to do so they pay half a shilling per day as a trader's tax. The money they receive from the sale of the milk which might amount to two or three shillings is normally spent in the market, or in one of the retail shops. In addition, the Masai provide the community with a fresh supply of meat through the local butchers' shops. Although some of the shopowners buy a few head of cattle at a time at the monthly cattle auctions held in Mto wa Mbu, these are not sufficient to meet the demand. The remaining beef is purchased from the odd Masai in the area who needs cash immediately. In return, the village is the center for a number of social services such as the dispensary and school which cater to the needs of the Masai as well as those of the residents of Mto wa Mbu.

Thus, the tie between Mto wa Mbu and the Masai is a formal one connecting two different types of communities. This has been reinforced by the reluctance of even a single Masai to establish residence in the village. The relationship between the residents of Mto wa Mbu and the neighboring Iraqw and Masai and to a lesser extent the more distant Wambugwe is similar. A major difference is that in recent years some Iraqw and Wambugwe have settled in the village. However, because of their close relationship to their nearby homes and a number of cultural traits, they are set apart in the eyes of other inhabitants as pseudo-residents of Mto wa Mbu.

In addition to a scarcity of social ties to the immediate outside area, the gap is widened by the attitudes which the respective inhabitants have toward each other. The Masai see the migrants to Mto wa Mbu as aliens in Masailand and do not recognize any cultural differences among them. To the Masai they are all grouped together and categorized as *Waswahili*. Although this is a vague and complicated term even in the academic literature, among the Masai it means simply any non-Masai agriculturalist in their territory. The residents of Mto wa Mbu also define themselves in this way as a means of distinguishing themselves from the Masai and to an extent from the Iraqw. However, to the people of Mto wa Mbu the term *Waswahili* also implies overtones of cultural superiority.

These two factors of social isolation and cultural distinctiveness vis-à-vis the surrounding groups have stimulated a sense of solidarity among the inhabitants of Mto wa Mbu. As stated, the Masai refer to the residents of Mto wa Mbu as *Waswahili* and the inhabitants accept this identification. The villagers, therefore, feel that there is something unique about their own way of life. Abrahams (1961) has tentatively suggested that a possible major factor of community integration in Kahama was the residents' adoption of a "Swahili culture." He candidly admits though that he is not quite sure what this entails. He can not be faulted for this because the label has a number of meanings, many of which are contradictory as both a folk and an anthropological category (Arens 1975a).

The Swahili people and culture have received much attention in the historical literature, but generally the subject has been treated without great concern for the social and cultural nuances of the term. In discussing the coast of East Africa under the jurisdiction of the Sultan of Zanzibar in the first half of the nineteenth century Coupland (1968:3) writes that the inhabitants of the towns were "Arabs or Swahili—the name of the mixed Arab and African race, which now far out numbered the dwindling remnant of pure Arabs, and of the similarly mixed language which had taken the place of Arabic along the maritime belt." The idea that there was a distinct group called the *Waswahili* is also accepted by Reusch (1953) who states that they formed a nation on the Tanzanian coast during the twelfth to sixteenth centuries.

Those social anthropologists who have carried out research on the East African coast such as Wijeyewardene (1958, 1959a, 1959b, and 1959c), Lienhardt (1968) and Prins (1967) have found matters to be much more complicated at least from the viewpoint of anthropological interests. For example, Lienhardt (1968) points out that recent arrivals to the coast from the Arabian peninsula are not called by the Swahili word normally translated as Arab (sing. *Mwarabu,* pl. *Waarabu*), but by two other terms depending upon whether they have come from Oman or the southern tip of the Arabian peninsula. On the other hand, the name *Waarabu* is applied to those individuals who claim Arab descent but whose families may have been living on the coast for centuries. This means that many of the individuals who are called *Waarabu* have adopted coastal manners and speak no Arabic. Further, adding to the confusion, he reports that for political reasons some people have claimed to be Africans after Tanzania and Kenya achieved independence while before they insisted that they were Arabs (Lienhardt 1968).

Needless to say the racial and ethnic situation on the coast of East Africa is a complex one with claims to status made and withdrawn depending upon the prevailing political currents. The problem of defining the term *Waswahili* is only slightly less confusing. In the anthopological literature with various degrees of reservation it is generally used to refer to individuals from the East African coast who speak Swahili, have a Muslim-Arab oriented culture and claim mixed Arab-African or mixed-ethnic descent (Gulliver 1959; Harries 1964; Omar 1940; and Tanner 1964). This is complicated by the fact that few people on the coast, at least until recently, would use the term *Mswahili* (sing.) as a means of self-identification since it is sometimes employed as a euphemism for descendants of slaves (Lienhardt 1968) and, therefore, implies social inferiority as well as the status of an alien.

The implications and vagueness surrounding this term has led to further complications. Hino (1968a) reports that in the usual sense the name Swahili originally referred to groups from the coast who used the Swahili language and had converted to Islam as a result of Arab influence in the area. However, he later states (Hino 1968b) that in the town of Ujiji on the inland extremity of Tanzania the inhabitants refer to the Muslim members of the community who originally came from Zaire as *Waswahili*. Wijeye-wardene (1959b) who has had the advantage of carrying out research on the East African coast points out that in one village a large number of individuals called themselves *Waswahili*. These people were mostly of slave descent, but also included recent immigrants from the interior such as Nyasa, Nyamwezi or Kamba or were members of distant coastal groups. It is interesting to note that in the interior, for example in Nyamwezi country, coastal people are called the *Waswahili*. Paradoxically, a Nyamwezi who is living on the coast would be called a *Mswahili* by the coastal people. It can also be assumed that the individuals themselves identify with this term in different ways. For example, a Nyamwezi living in his traditional home would call himself a Nyamwezi but while on the coast he would call himself a *Mswahili*. The reverse would also be true for a coastal resident since he would not claim to be a *Mswahili* at home, but would do so in Nyamwezi country.

The problem is further complicated by Wazaki's (1966) and Ishige's (1969) reports on the poly-ethnic village of Mongola a short distance from Mto wa Mbu in Mbulu District. They state that the migrants who have come to settle there from other parts of Tanzania call themselves *Waswahili*. They both argue that this is based on the use of the Swahili language by the inhabitants, but also is an attempt to set themselves off as a distinct group from the surrounding Iraqw and Barabaig which parallels the situation in Mto wa Mbu.

Despite this confusion the term Swahili has some basic cultural connotations, the most basic being the use of the Swahili language.

More important, a *Mswahili* is one who occupies a specific status in an area which in turn might necessitate the use of a specific cultural item. For example, a migrant will be forced to use *kiswahili* since it is a lingua franca and a number of individuals from various ethnic groups in a single place will by necessity employ it. In this situation, all foreigners in an area occupy a single status, make use of the same cultural items and as a result are seen by others and themselves as a distinct group. Such is the case with Mto wa Mbu, and, therefore, it is a Swahili community in the minds of all concerned, both residents and outsiders.

In addition to the fact that the term Swahili is used as a term of identification in the context of spatial location, it also has various connotations with regard to prestige. As has been shown, on the coast as a term of reference it implies a socially and culturally inferior group composed of former slaves or members of interior groups. Prins (1967) also reports that on the islands off the coast, including Zanzibar, the term is never used as a means of self-identification. However, "people of higher social strata in any given community readily refer to their inferiors as Swahili" (1967: 11).

Again, this can be contrasted with the meaning of Swahili in Mto wa Mbu and in other interior poly-ethnic villages where it connotes cultural superiority in opposition to the supposed inferior status of the surrounding inhabitants. The opportunity to distinguish themselves as a superior group is readily provided for the residents of Mto wa Mbu by the proximity of the Masai and the Iraqw who frequent the village on a daily basis. Neither of these two groups are Bantu and consequently they provide a number of readily discernible characteristics, including to a certain extent their physical features, which set them apart from the residents. More important to the villagers, both groups represent an archaic way of life. This includes a greater reliance on their own language and in many cases an almost complete ignorance of *Kiswahili*. Further, these languages being non-Bantu strike the residents as completely foreign to *Kiswahili* and their own mother tongues. As an indication, in *Kiswahili* the Iraqw are called the *Wambulu* which literally means people who say meaningless or unintelligible things. Other factors such as a disregard for both Islam and Christianity, the wearing of cloaks and beads, and carrying spears by the Masai and Iraqw contribute to the feeling of distinctiveness on the part of the people of Mto wa Mbu. In general, the town dwellers see these two groups as representing an extremely different type of cultural tradition from their own. They conceive of their Swahili culture as being more modern and sophisticated, and, therefore, superior to that of the surrounding people.

The term *Waswahili* also has other meanings when used by the residents as a means of identification within the community itself; but, when used vis-à-vis the immediate outside world, it is a category of reference which includes all residents of Mto wa Mbu.

Since it has been mentioned that the Swahili language is a basic characteristic of the cultural category something should be said about its function in Mto wa Mbu. Considering the mixture of ethnic groups represented and the number of possible languages, without the use of the *Kiswahili* the community would rival the scene around the mythical Tower of Babel. All four of the major African language families are spoken by members of the village as indicated by the presence of traditional Bantu, Para Nilotic, Cushitic and Khoisan speakers. The existence of language speakers of each type clustered together in a nearby district which has provided migrants to the settlement is the primary cause of the diversity of mother tongues. However, the great majority of the inhabitants were traditional Bantu speakers.

This diversity of traditional languages means that *Kiswahili* is a major factor of cultural integration. Regardless of origin, all the inhabitants are fluent in the dialect, and it is rare that one hears the use of other languages in public places, except for occasional greetings. The degree of fluency in *Kiswahili* varies with individual speakers and groups. Those people from the coast where *Kiswahili* is the first language or it is rapidly surpassing the traditional one and those with a fair degree of education have a greater mastery of the language than others. In the latter category would fall those individuals from areas where *Kiswahili* has been of less importance than the traditional tongue.

Because of this variance in the fluency among groups, *Kiswahili* also serves as a means of division in the community, since for the residence a good grasp of vocabulary and grammar is considered a sign of progressiveness and superiority. On the other hand, individuals and groups lacking this skill are considered backward and uncouth, so that it is said by some that certain people in the village *"wanaharibu Kiswahili"* (debase Swahili) by their ignorance of its finer points.

Although *Kiswahili* is spoken by everyone, the traditional languages continue to be used in certain contexts and serve as a means of emphasizing and reinforcing the solidarity between individuals with a common cultural heritage. Individuals from the same ethnic group use their own language in preference to *Kiswahili* when together, even occasionally in public, if they have something private to discuss. However, if a third party who does not understand the language joins the group, *Kiswahili* is quickly substituted.

If a few individuals use their traditional tongue in public, someone else is bound to comment on this and inquire why they are speaking a language unintelligible to others. Since the prevailing attitude in such a situation is that everyone else's traditional tongue is gibberish, ridicule often follows. This would include a good-natured, but generally negative, analysis of the group in question.

In an attempt to attempt to assess the importance of *Kiswahili*, the question was included in the household survey, which indicated that, in close to half of them (44 percent), only *Kiswahili* was used. In most of the remaining houses (45 percent), the traditional language was mainly spoken, with the *lingua franca* used secondarily. In a small proportion (10 percent), only the traditional language was employed. Where *Kiswahili* was the only language spoken, the husband and wife were usually from different ethnic groups.

The data on the children's linguistic ability showed that almost three-quarters (73 percent) had a knowledge of their parents' language. In some instances this involved not only one but two dialects, with varying proficiency. Where the parents were of different ethnic groups, the child's mastery might include only a few words or phrases, while if they were of the same, it might mean fluency.

The data indicate that although *Kiswahili* may be the language of the community, it has by no means replaced the traditional ones. Nevertheless, the fact that in almost half of the households only *Kiswahili* is spoken indicates its importance. As the number of inter-ethnic marriages increases, which is the apparent trend, the number of households where only *Kiswahili* is spoken will also increase.

INTERNAL DIVISIONS

The preceding discussion concedes the fact that the village of Mto wa Mbu and its residents exhibit a degree of internal cohesion as a reaction to external factors and shared cultural traits. However, there are also various internal stresses and strains which divide the community. The internal divisions from the standpoint of both the inhabitants and the outside observer will be examined at this juncture as well as the manner in which internal cohesion is maintained on the basis of community-wide organizations.

In considering possible lines of cleavage within Mto wa Mbu the significance of "tribalism" must be evaluated since it is an obvious and often discussed topic in studies of poly-ethnic urban centers. This subject was raised earlier and discussed from the standpoint of community ideology and values which deny the existence of discrete ethnic units as a feature of social organization. The objective reasons for their unimportance to the internal structure of the village is another matter and prompts other considerations.

The simplest explanation is that such groups could not function in any meaningful way for their potential membership. In some instances a number of people with the same background may be represented by three or four hundred residents while another by only one or two households totalling ten people. In the latter example it is impossible to interact, much less to establish minimal social relationships within an ethnic boundary. Identification with a larger group on this basis is equally impossible since for numerical reasons it does not exist. Since so many of the inhabitants' traditional group are represented by less than one or two per cent of the population, this is not an insignificant factor. Consequently, if an individual says, for example, that he is a Nyasa, he is referring to a category of people which exists beyond the limits of Mto wa Mbu. By the same token if in conversation the same person were described by others as *yule Mnyasa* (that Nyasa) it implies something about him in relation to a group of people called the *Wanyasa* who live in Southern Tanzania. In effect, an ethnic label is a means of identification within the community on the basis of an external category, but it does not connote a social group within Mto wa Mbu. The same conditions hold true for those whose ethnic group may form a greater segment of the population.

Thus, the mere existence of so many possible categories prevents the emergence of the group as a feasible factor in community organization. If the number were significantly less and each had stronger representation, then this might not be the case. Ideology might state that "tribalism" should not be thought of but it is the demographic reality of the local situation which also makes it unthinkable.

This does not mean that an individual does not occasionally seek out co-ethnics or find comfort or self-identification through spending some time with them using the traditional language. However, this can not and does not lead to the formation of a larger complex of social relationships of a closed or even semi-closed nature. The demands of everyday living which necessitate the creation of crucial social relationships across ethnic lines militate against the development of important social groupings based on common origin. The composition of the village itself in the form of numerous ethnic affiliations works against this. In order for social interaction to take place on a community-wide level and with the degree of cooperation required by irrigation agriculture, ethnic consciousness must be submerged.

The validity of this argument may appear to be weakened by the peculiar case provided by the Chagga. However, it is the initial unique economic interest of the Chagga in the community which is not shared by others which provides an explanation for the significance of ethnicity among them. They are the exception to the rule because they are not the typical settler. Consequently, to identify an individual as a Chagga is a meaningful statement about his membership in a viable group within the community (Arens 1973).

Except for this single case ethnicity fails to play an important role in the creation of internal divisions within the village. However, ethnic affiliation is one of the factors in the emergence of larger socio-cultural units. These divisions become apparent from discussions with residents on the subject of the kinds of people who are living in the community and the distinctions between them. Such differences also become clear on the basis of the observation of the behavior of the residents which leads to the possibility of distinguishing broad social and cultural segments in which traditional identity does play a part.

Although unnamed and unrecognized by the villagers, it is possible to construct such a model of the community. What follows, therefore, is essentially a model which is not recognized explicitly by the residents themselves. This might be made more concrete from a conversation with the local party chairman who is one of the most perceptive men in the village. In a general discussion on how the party was organized I pointed out that he as well as all of the previous chairmen were Muslims. When I asked if this was because a candidate would have to be a Muslim in order to be elected, he replied in the negative. He commented that there were Christians and Muslims in Mto wa Mbu, but more of the latter so that a Muslim became chairman. But, he added, religion had nothing to do with politics. His own values as well as political office prevent the outright expression of the existence of divisions in the community along religious lines although they may be recognized by everyone. However, the statement that there are Muslims and Christians in the village is clear enough. If this can be correlated with similar factors such as a system of prestige stratification, a distinct outline is perceptible which provides a useful device for an understanding of community organization (Arens 1975b).

With this in mind, it is possible to construct a tripartite typology which incorporates the community's population into a number of groups based on a limited set of factors. The individuals from along the coastal belt who share a number of common cultural traits, such as Islam, and who were among the first settlers of the village, illustrate such a type. The tendency to identify with each other, regardless of other differences, and to restrict many voluntary relationships amongst themselves underscores the social significance of this merging process.

This corresponds to the way in which the residents themselves see their community. Their perception of the unified nature of the village exists only in relation to the outside world. In this sense they are a single people, but within the community they also recognize different kinds of residents. This allows for a conception of village organization along simple lines not made possible from a restricted ethnic perspective. Although not named by the residents themselves, the following categories are distinguished: the Coastal Swahili, the Interior Swahili, and the Christian-Progressive.

The Coastal Swahili. These individuals are represented by members of a number of coastal or near coastal tribes such as the Zigua, Zaramo, Segeju and Sambaa. They are the bearers of a cultural tradition involving a mixture of Arab and African components epitomized by adherence to Islam and the use of *Kiswahili* as their first language. They conceive of themselves as a culturally superior group in the community, especially with regard to those people from inland areas who have adopted Islam at a later date.

In Mto wa Mbu they feel that they provide the community with its cultural character since in many ways it bears a resemblance to that of the East African littoral with Islam as the predominant religion and *Kiswahili* as the means of communication among all inhabitants. The type of dress originating on the coast such as the *kanzu* (a long gown extending from neck to ankles) and *kofia* (Muslim cap) which has been adopted by a number of the other residents further supports the contention of the Coastal Swahili that they have provided a cultural tradition which has subordinated an inferior one.

Within the village, these residents share a distinct cultural bond which although originating outside of the community has been transplanted and maintained successfully within Mto wa Mbu. Two individuals from the coast, even though one is from Kenya and the other from Tanzania, see themselves more closely related to each other than to their fellow countrymen from different areas. It is not geography alone, but rather a recognition of shared customs, historical tradition and very likely a common set of experiences within their own lifetimes which provide the stimuli. Many of these individuals, especially those from the Tanzanian coast, were directly involved in the colonial social system in some manner. They, or at least the original migrants of this group, were among the first settlers of Mto wa Mbu and brought with them a language and religion which gave a sense of solidarity and cultural substance to the community through the sharing of these common items.

Within Mto wa Mbu these individuals, especially the older residents, are accorded a great deal of prestige by other segments of the Muslim population. They have been important agents in converting many other members to Islam and are recognized by the Muslims as the source of strength of the Islamic community. However, as indicated they consider co-religionists from inland zones to be somewhat culturally inferior bearers of a diluted Swahili culture. This is constantly reinforced by the fact that many of these individuals from the interior who have converted do not adhere as strictly to Islamic practices as the coastal group. As a consequence they are looked down upon for failing to abstain from the drinking of alcoholic beverages or for their infrequent attendance at daily prayers.

The coastal group also considers itself to be superior to the Christians in residence, but as is to be expected, the Christians do not reciprocate by according this status to them. The coastal Muslims see the Christians as falling outside of the system of prestige ranking on the basis of religion alone while the Christians see all Muslims in many ways as the representatives of an archaic cultural tradition.

The Interior Swahili. This type of resident is seen to be closely related to the Coastal Swahili and is exemplified by representatives from the Rangi, Iramba and Gogo. The traditional homes of individuals from these groups are in the general Central Tanzania area along former trade routes or around what later became important colonial centers. As a result, these groups have been in contact with and affected by external influences. They have had an Islamic tradition for a period of time although slight in comparison to the coastal group with which they seek to identify.

Some of the residents in the village from this group are Muslims by birth although most have been converted to Islam during their travels or after settling in Mto wa Mbu. Their arrival in the community was normally preceded by a period of migration and wage labor in European centers or colonial government projects. The fact that they were low paid, unskilled laborers rarely having even a minimum of religious or secular education, and accepted Islam at a later date, earned them a special position in the community. These individuals have migrated to Mto wa Mbu over a long period of time and their interest in the community is purely agricultural with few engaging in any serious trading activities. During the course of their residence in Mto wa Mbu they have modelled their behavior after the coastal group to the extent of adapting coastal habits of dress as well as religion. However, because of their common cultural bond and their similar experiences as migrants, they are set apart from the Coastal Swahili.

The Christian-Progressive. These individuals are illustrated by the Christian segment of the population who have arrived as a group most recently and have taken a greater interest in trading possibilities in Mto wa Mbu. This type is most clearly exemplified by the Chagga and the Pare residents. It is not only religion, however, which separates them from the rest of the population, but also the fact that they consider themselves more progressive, modern and educated than their fellow residents in Mto wa Mbu and their economic behavior is seen as a testament to this belief. Their style of clothing is European and they have an equal disdain for the Muslim dress and the traditional costume of the Masai which they consider outdated. As a group their proficiency in *Kiswahili* is equal to that of the former coastal residents. However, it does not represent a traditional cultural heritage, but an educational attainment since the language of instruction in Tanzanian primary schools is *Kiswahili*. These individuals show a great interest in events outside of Mto wa Mbu through newspapers and the radio and consider others in the community backward and provincial. Except for the government officials, it is only among this group that any knowledge of English is displayed as another indication of their educational attainment.

Since they have arrived in· large numbers recently because of overpopulation and lack of economic opportunities in their own fertile homeland, they do not see Mto wa Mbu as a great step upward for themselves. If given the opportunity they would return home since they have been pushed, rather than pulled, into Mto wa Mbu. As a result, they see it as a place to exploit economically either through agriculture or trade until a better opportunity arrives or a chance to return home. This combination of characteristics and outlook sets them apart from the Coastal Swahili and Interior Swahili.

The inclusiveness of the typology is attested to by its applicability to the government employees posted to the area. In Mto wa Mbu there is little to say about a system of socio-economic stratification since the overwhelming majority of the inhabitants are small-scale cultivators. The government officials in Mto wa Mbu do not form a distinct category and are never referred to as *wageni* (strangers). Instead, they are absorbed into the community structure and participate in it. For example, the two magistrates of the local court who are Muslims take part fully in Islamic affairs, such as holidays and marriages or deaths, and are seen primarily as members of the Coastal Swahili group and not as members of an elite based on education, occupation or income. The same situation would hold for other officials who may be Christian, such as the head teacher in the primary school or a community development officer. In short, such possible distinctions are submerged in the typology described. More detailed discussions of marriage, kinship and the kind of orientations which residents display toward Mto wa Mbu will indicate more clearly the importance of the factors involved which support this typology.

It is necessary to re-emphasize that although ethnicity may be a feature of this system of classification it is not the only factor nor the most significant one. Education, occupation and religion are equal, if not more important, considerations. Consequently, to label these groups as the equivalent of urban "super-tribes" (Mitchell 1956) would be seriously misleading. In Mto wa Mbu neither ethnic groups nor "super-tribes" are features of village social organization.

RELIGION

Mto wa Mbu like other densely settled communities in Tanzania is predominantly Muslim. According to the 1967 census the village had a religious composition of 59.7 percent Muslim, 32.2 percent Christian and 8.5 percent express no preference. However, the Iraqw who are really part-time residents form a large portion of this latter figure of traditionalists. The Wambugwe in the village, whose original home is also a short distance away, also figure highly in this percentage and to an extent their relationship in Mto wa Mbu is similar to that of the Iraqw.

The number of long-term residents from more distant areas who have failed to convert to Islam or Christianity is, therefore, fairly small. Although few in number they play an important role in Mto wa Mbu since they are looked upon as reservoirs of traditional knowledge and practices. Many of these individuals act as diviners in cases where sorcery is suspected and are the suppliers of folk medicine to counteract illness attributed to both natural and supernatural agents of misfortune. Their clients are either traditionalists, Christians or Muslims. However, Muslims, especially those from the coast, avail themselves of these services to a limited degree since Islam in East Africa allows for intervention of supernatural and malicious agents which can be counteracted within the framework of Islamic doctrine and practices. In East African Islam the *mwalimu* (teacher) normally is both religious cleric as well as diviner and treater of illness through medicines (Trimingham 1964). Further, the system of religious beliefs includes the recognition of possessive spirits causing mental and physical harm which can be counteracted by orthodox ritual (Lewis 1966).

Religious affiliation is significant in Mto wa Mbu since it plays a more important role in the life of the resident than it would if he were living in his traditional home. At home in the company of fellow ethnics, Christianity or Islam may be a relatively inconsequential aspect of social identification and unimportant in establishing social relationships as compared to other social factors. Consequently, in studying a traditional society it might be feasible to overlook religious orientation as an important aspect of social structure because in such a situation the individuals fail to consider themselves primarily either Christians or Muslims. However, in Mto wa Mbu where traditional groups are not functioning and ethnic groups are unimportant the residents have come to rely on their religion as a more important means of identification and source of values.

Religion in Mto wa Mbu diminishes the importance of ethnic ties and provides the means for establishing links across these lines. In many instances ethnic and religious identity may coincide. In such cases an already existing feeling of solidarity is reinforced. However, this does not work out so neatly in all instances since individuals from the same ethnic group may have different religious preferences so that some are Christian while others are Muslims. As a result, a number of individuals may identify with one segment of the population on the basis of traditional cultural similarities while identifying with another through religion. Such a situation may involve a certain amount of conflict for the individual in terms of self-identification and loyalties, but for the community it has the opposite effect of uniting larger groups through the existence of these dual loyalties. Religion, therefore, not only divides the community, but also functions to unite it at other points. Further, for those residents who are members of an ethnic group insignificantly represented in the population, religion provides the opportunity for identification with a larger group within the community.

The relationship between the Muslim and Christian population is never expressed in overt hostility or in terms of the formation of clear-cut groupings over explicit issues. Yet, in less obvious situations such as informal social behavior, marketing and trade transactions or with friendship relationships and marriage it becomes clear that behavior often takes place across ethnic lines but within religious ones. In addition, the religious groups often exhibit uncomplimentary attitudes toward each other. For example, the Christians are quite willing to admit that they feel it is difficult to do business with Muslims since they can not be trusted, or to generally point out the absurdity of Muslim customs as compared to their own. A particular point of ridicule often commented upon concerns Muslim marriage practices. Since Muslims may marry for a few hundred shillings in bride wealth and the wedding celebration normally involves serving only tea and cakes to the guests, this is an indication to the Christians of the little value which Muslims place on marriage as well as on the friends and kinsmen who have come to celebrate the event. As one Christian pointed out, some Muslims marry for the price of a goat (30 to 50 shillings). Also, in the Christian's view the idea of middle-aged and old Muslim men marrying teenage girls is particularly repulsive and an indication of an unhealthy sexual attitude.

Finally, the Christians consider the Muslims as backward for their failure to be interested in anything more than cultivating their fields. The Muslim value of religious over secular education is also criticized. Although the community is almost two-thirds (64 percent) Muslim, the Christian children in the primary school where attendance is theoretically compulsory outnumber the Muslims by a small percentage.

The Muslims in turn view the Christians as overly aggressive in economic transactions and prefer to deal when possible with co-religionists in the market. According to the Muslims this desire for money has led to the opening of numerous drinking places under Christian ownership and has affected the moral climate of the community. The majority of the patrons and the girls who work in these bars as waitresses are Christians which supports the Muslim contention that vice is rampant among the Christian population.

The significance of religious differences is overtly expressed on ritual occasions. Both marriages and funerals are largely public affairs which take place in full view of neighbors and passers-by. Normally those neighbors and acquaintances of a different religion than the principals will make an appearance at some time during the proceedings, but remain only briefly and on the periphery of the assembly. On one occasion while paying my respects to the family of a respected Muslim member of the village who had just died and planning to remain I was told by a Christian informant who had accompanied me that we should not stay for "this was not our place." As is to be expected, religious segregation continues in death as in life as reflected by the use of separate burial sites for Muslims and Christians.

This discussion has slightly oversimplified the situation since the Christian population is subdivided into a number of different congregations which include Lutherans, Roman Catholics and a small number of Seventh Day Adventists. However, more important is that Christianity, even among members of the same sect, does not foster the same degree of solidarity across ethnic lines as Islam. The sharing of Islam is more significant among Muslims than any possible differences engendered by divergent ethnic backgrounds. The reasons for this can be appreciated by an analysis of some of the basic differences between the expression of Islam and Christianity in East Africa.

First it is necessary to return to the question of why the population centers in Tanzania, both rural and urban, are predominantly Muslim. Mto wa Mbu with a Muslim majority is surrounded by the scattered homesteads of the Masai and Iraqw who have generally retained their traditional beliefs. The few who have not are more than likely Christians. Abrahams (1961) reports that in Kahama township almost three-quarters (71 percent) of his sample claimed to be Muslims which was again a contrast to the religious orientation of the countryside. Further, even a casual visit to any small settlement in the countryside bears out the assumption that the majority of the residents are Muslims. In Tanzania, therefore, Islam is the religion of the more compact centers which are composed of migrants. This situation can be compared to the fact that Muslims make up only about one-quarter of the Tanzanian population (Trimingham 1968).

The reason for this is both historical and social. Islam was the first world religion to penetrate East Africa via the coastal islands and subsequently gained a foothold on the coast in the twelfth century (Trimingham 1968). The establishment of coastal trading centers by the Arabs during this era and their inter-marriage with the local population resulted in the implantation of Islam centuries before the arrival of the Europeans and Christianity. Islam spread to a lesser degree along the interior trade routes and became the established religion of the few inland settlements and was then accepted to some extent by the adjacent groups. Therefore, by the advent of the European period Islam had a long tradition as the religion of small and large population centers of mainland Tanzania and had adapted itself to the characteristics of town life with its concurrent mixture of various ethnic and racial groups.

Another and paradoxical factor contributing to the spread of Islam in Tanzania which was commented on briefly before was the arrival of the Germans on the coast in the late nineteenth century and their subsequent movement into the interior. During the process of setting up a colonial administrative structure, the Germans relied heavily on African personnel from the coastal area who were Muslims. These individuals accompanied the Europeans into the interior where they took up residence at the administrative centers. The result was the spread of Islam through conversion to areas which previously had been untouched by Muslim influence (Trimingham 1968). Consequently, rather than acting solely as agents for the transmission of Christianity, the Germans also provided the stimulus and network for the spread of Islamic influence. As a consequence, by the early twentieth century Islam and other coastal cultural characteristics, such as modes of dress and *Kiswahili,* became a characteristic feature of town life in Tanzania, far from the maritime belt.

However, not only historical factors account for the predominance of Muslims in settlements, since there are also cultural and social aspects of Islam which are particularly suited to the polyethnic town. In Mto wa Mbu, Islam serves to break down certain barriers between individuals of different backgrounds in a way that Christianity does not. Islam involves more than an acceptance of a set of ideas concerning the supernatural, for it also means adopting a particular life-style, including dietary habits, mode of dress, and a set of uniform customs regulating marriage, descent and inheritance. Thus, Islam has not superseded traditions, rather it has often incorporated these practices and beliefs within its framework. General surveys on Islam in Africa have commented on its adaptability to existing systems of beliefs and related practices (Trimingham 1964; Lewis 1966; Horton 1971). Although the conclusions must be treated with care, the conversion process has clearly resulted in the emergence of a common Islamic element with regard to ideas and behavior.

The same might also be argued for Christianity, since all adherents, regardless of ethnic origin, ideally subscribe to a common prescribed set of ideas and rituals. However, the crucial distinction between Islam and Christianity is that the latter often attempts to supplant indigenous beliefs and customs. The result of this dogmatism is that Christianity does not replace traditional ideas and practices but exists parallel with them. Christianity, therefore, by merely presenting an alternative, in effect encourages the retention of diverse and distinctive customs of a traditional nature among its own adherents. Consequently, as will be shown, one can be married as both a Christian and according to traditional practice. On the other hand, a Muslim can be and is only married as a Muslim although some traditional elements may be incorporated into the ceremony.

Since Christianity attempts to establish a new set of beliefs without the same regard for the traditional ones as Islam, it also entails the rejection of certain cultural items without replacing them with others. Islam, to cite just one example, allows for the belief in witches and sorcerers and in doing so also provides the means as well as the functionaries for combating these perceived evils. Christianity conversely does not allow for these agents and cannot combat them. This means that a Muslim can react under these circumstances as a Muslim while a Christian must respond not as a member of his faith but in a manner prescribed by traditional beliefs.

To summarize, Islam provides a holistic ethos by permitting adherents to act as Muslims in a greater variety of situations and encourages religious identification in a greater number of instances. The specific Muslim reaction to birth, death, marriage or to the ancestors, witches and sorcerers creates a bond amongst its members through the acceptance of a basic set of common ideas and rituals. Christianity, on the other hand, is severely limited in this regard and pervades only a partial aspect of an individual's behavior, beliefs and identification (Arens 1975b).

The easiest way to explain this sense of community is to describe the events of two inter-ethnic marriages, one involving Muslims and the other Christians. In the Muslim case, the man was a middle-aged Segeju, who had recently divorced his first wife, and the bride was a young Rangi woman. On the morning of the marriage day, the groom, who was also a local Muslim teacher, was escorted to the bride's house by his friends, as well as the children from the Muslim school, singing Arabic and *Kiswahili* songs. They were met at the bride's house by her father and his contingent. The groom and the girl's father sat facing each other in the presence of a second Muslim cleric who officiated. The cleric stated the particulars of the marriage contract, including the bride price, the amount already paid and the amount remaining. He then asked the groom if he agreed to these conditions. The same contract was repeated for the father of the bride and his assent was sought and given. Following this brief exchange the groom and witnesses entered the house and asked for the bride's consent to the marriage. Having received it he returned outside again where he, her father, and the cleric signed the marriage contract containing all of the particulars which were previously stated orally. At that point the couple were officially married although the ceremony was not at an end.

The groom and his company then returned home for a meal. In the early afternoon the bride's kinsmen and friends arrived at the groom's house with the marriage presents which the young girl had received as part of her dowry and then they left. A short time later they returned again with the bride who seated on a bicycle was being pushed along by the males of the party. Her face and body were completely hidden by a black garment (buibui) which covered her from head to foot. The bride was then carried into the house and presented to her husband and the crowd dispersed.

Later that evening the bride's two married sisters and her mother's sister returned to the groom's home to collect the blood-stained sheet which was proof of the bride's virginity. The sheet was presented to her kinsmen by a woman called a soma who according to Islamic custom lives with the new couple for seven days doing the chores usually performed by the wife. Having received the proof of the bride's virginity, her kinsmen began to sing traditional marriage songs of the Rangi. They then returned to the bride's former home where they were met by the girl's mother and her neighbors. The singing of songs and dancing by the women continued for a few hours and then broke up.

The important point is that the marriage itself included only Islamic customs. It was not until the marriage had already been consummated that any elements of Rangi culture in the form of dancing and singing were introduced. The marriage ceremony and the contract were completely Islamic or at least Islamic-East African syncretisms. This can be compared to a typical marriage between two Christians.

The couple, the husband an Ikoma and the wife a Pare, were already married two years before in a Protestant and traditional ceremony at his home. At that time he had promised his wife and her parents that at a later date when he was financially able he would marry according to a traditional ceremony at her village in Pare country.

It is difficult to describe the confusion that reigned during the day of the wedding. The "bride" had arrived a few days before her husband and he was told that according to Pare custom he was unable to see her. When he inquired of her kinsmen the customs and type of ceremony for the marriage on the next day, he was met with blank stares. As a consequence, he was fined a number of times by the girl's kinsmen for failing to abide by Pare customs.

The marriage itself did not seem very traditional in many ways. The bride wore a white wedding gown and the groom a dark suit. The ceremony involved the groom and his companions meeting the bride at the door of her house in the company of her female kinsmen and leading her out. This was followed by a few songs in *Kiswahili* and a poem in the Pare language written for the occasion.

The fact that the wife's kinsmen demanded that a Pare wedding take place after the religious one of two years before is significant in itself. Also, to the observer it was obvious that the groom was considered by the bride's family and friends in her village to be a complete outsider. The notion that they were all members of the same religion was secondary to the fact that he was not a Pare. There was none of the solidarity that is observed among Muslims of different backgrounds under the same conditions. It might be argued that the Pare treat all bridegrooms in the same way. However, the groom's stranger and inferior status was magnified by the fact that he was from a foreign group.

Further, for the Muslims, as indicated by the first example, Islamic custom takes precedence over the traditional culture. As a consequence, Islamic law regarding divorce, descent and inheritance as well as marriage is the norm adhered to by all Muslims. The result is a religious community and a weakening of potential divisions. Obviously, in traditional societies where Islam has had some degree of impact this might not be the case. However, in a community like Mto wa Mbu where the inhabitants have divorced themselves to a great extent both physically and socially from their traditional homes, the influence of Islam as a mechanism of integration can not be underestimated.

This cultural uniformity which Islam stimulates is, however, only a part of the picture for in addition the Muslim community has certain structural features extremely well suited to town life which support religious values, beliefs and practices. Of particular importance is the role of the Muslim teacher or *mwalimu*. All

Muslims are expected through study to attain some degree of knowledge concerning the rites, prayers, customs and laws of Islam. Those individuals who continue on with their religious studies under the supervision of a *mwalimu* can also attain this respected status and title. Although there is a degree of variation in terms of proficiency within the ranks of these teachers, the lowest common denominator is the ability to recite the Koran in Arabic and the memorization of the important prayers. Comprehension of what is read in Arabic varies from individual to individual.

The relative ease in attaining this status and the ability of one teacher to train others insures that in any community there will be at least one *mwalimu* and usually more in residence. In Mto wa Mbu with approximately 2,000 Muslims there were ten Muslim teachers. Therefore, in every community there will be at least one representative who can speak with some degree of authority on Islamic laws and customs to whom disputes concerning marriage, divorce, and inheritance can be taken for adjudication regardless of the cultural background of the litigants. In some communities as was the case in Mto wa Mbu there may also be a Muslim court where a number of the respected men in the village come together to listen to disputes and recommend settlements. At the present time, this institution seems to be of little importance, but it was frequently used before the establishment of a government primary court. Nevertheless, one of the most learned Muslim teachers in Mto wa Mbu is frequently called upon by the government magistrates to give advice with regard to Islamic law and its possible application in cases involving Muslims.

The presence of a *mwalimu* also means that the Muslim children in the community receive religious instruction and this insures that even if the children do not receive a secular education they have a knowledge of Islam and some ability to write *Kiswahili* in Arabic script. This can be compared with the Christian sects which have no such arrangement but rely on the religious instruction which is allowed in the government school under the direction of the evangelists from the Christian churches.

In Mto wa Mbu these factors have resulted in Islam establishing and maintaining itself as the predominant religion. The existence of a *mwalimu*, a mosque, school and court from the earliest days has meant the introduction of a community structure on an Islamic basis to counteract the possible dispersive forces. Further, this religious-jural organization has acted as a powerful magnet in attracting converts to Islam. As new settlers sought to establish themselves in Mto wa Mbu where kinship ties were lacking and those based on ethnicity might serve to isolate rather than to integrate, the conversion to Islam provided a significant means of contracting binding ties with established residents.

6

THE POLITICS OF UNITY

In the previous section the discussion examined: (1) the manner in which Mto wa Mbu reflects a unified community in relation to the outside world; and (2) how at the same time it is divided internally on the basis of broad cultural divisions and religious groups. It remains to consider separately the role of the local party structure as it serves to re-unite the residents on the basis of participation in a single organization and the acceptance of a common political ideology. Although this organization is an imposed one and implemented on the basis of national party directives, it will become apparent from a consideration of its emergence and function that the party is an integral part of the structure of the community.

In addition, this chapter will seek to determine why voluntary associations, so prevalent in urban areas, have failed to develop in Mto wa Mbu. Although this will involve the consideration of a social phenomenon absent in Mto wa Mbu, the discussion will shed some further light on the insignificance of ethnic affiliation and indicate one of the major differences between rural and urban poly-ethnic centers.

TANU

An outline of the contemporary political system in mainland Tanzania will set the stage for an appreciation of its role in Mto wa Mbu. First, Tanzania is a single party state and the Tanganyika African National Union (TANU) is the sole legitimate party since the constitutional revisions of 1965. Second, the TANU organization is interwoven with the government administration and takes precedence over it in the sense that according to the prevailing ideology the government is the servant of the people and their party. Third, the party organization reaches down to the roots of the country through a system of party cells and cell leaders. The intended purpose of this cell organization is to serve as a channel of communication on party issues, but in Mto wa Mbu it has taken on many other important functions.

The Mto wa Mbu branch of TANU was established in 1955 and was the first in the entire District. The traditional groups in the area such as the Masai, Iraqw, and Wambugwe took very little interest in national political affairs, but the residents of Mto wa Mbu have done so from the early days of the independence movement. Interestingly enough the first chairman was originally a Kissii from Kenya who was then living in Mto wa Mbu. The TANU office in Mto wa Mbu also served as the headquarters for organizing party activities in the surrounding country. However, its attempts met with success only in the other alien settlements in the area.

The response of the residents of Mto wa Mbu to TANU was not unique since Bienen (1967) has reported that the party attracted ethnic minorities living outside of their homes in all parts of Tanzania. These "strangers" normally found in isolated and relatively compact settlements became the carriers of the new political culture of the nation (Bienen 1967). Such a description adequately characterizes Mto wa Mbu and its political function.

Another interesting aspect of the establishment of the party is that in the pre-independence era its organizers and supporters were involved in an anti-sorcery movement in the community. During fieldwork it was difficult to reconstruct the actual events and ascertain who the main participants were in terms of supporting or actively discouraging the movement. At the time the supporters of the anti-sorcery campaign were associated with TANU while those discouraging it were not. Therefore, at the time of fieldwork no one was willing to admit that he opposed the movement since it was an indication of an earlier opposition to the party in the village. Individuals named by others as having refused to participate in the campaign now claim to have played an active part.

Nevertheless, the following seems to be the most agreed upon version and the most probable from a sociological standpoint. In 1959 an individual called Nguvumali[1] appeared in the community and told some acquaintances he could rid Mto wa Mbu of sorcerers. Those individuals who were younger men and also supporters of TANU actively encouraged the testing of all residents by submitting them to the medicines of Nguvumali. Opposed to this scheme were the British appointed *jumbe* (headman) and his assistants as well as a number of older influential and respected residents of the community. However, public opinion supported the search for the sorcerers in their midst and over a period of days hundreds voluntarily submitted themselves to the drinking of a mixture prepared by Nguvumali in order to prove their innocence. Unfortunately for many, their claims were negated by their violent reaction to the potion. These individuals were forced to pay a fine of ten shillings for practicing sorcery and for a medicine which would then render their powers impotent. Many others refused to submit to the test and thereby earned the reputation of unrepentent evil doers. This group included a number of formerly highly respected residents and government agents. As their status in the community was reduced that of the organizers and TANU was increased.

This anti-sorcery movement of 1959 in Mto wa Mbu closely parallels a description of a similar movement called "Kamcape" reported by Willis (1968) among the Fipa of Tanzania in 1963-1964. He reports that prominent backers of this movement in Ufipa were the younger men and women supporters of TANU who were also blocked in their economic aspirations by their elders and the traditional system of authority. He felt that the movement was an outlet for the conflict produced by the structure of Fipa society but did not indicate a radical or permanent change in the traditional political system. Parkin has taken issue with this interpretation and suggests "that internal role changes were always advertised in these movements" (Parkin 1968:426). This suggestion seems to find support with the material from Mto wa Mbu since the event did indicate a change in the source of authority from British appointed officials to local TANU leaders in the community. Among the Fipa the challenge was made after independence in recognition of the strength of the traditional system. However, in Mto wa Mbu it occurred prior to independence since the existing authority structure had minimal legitimacy. The anti-sorcery movement in Mto wa Mbu reflected the early strength of TANU in opposition to outside sources of authority which were foreign in nature.

This argument is strengthened by recognition of the ease with which the party took hold in the village. According to the first chairman implanting the party in the village was a relatively simple task. He first heard about TANU while visiting Arusha and decided to attend one of their meetings and returned to Mto wa Mbu with their message. He said at the time the inhabitants of Mto wa Mbu were ignorant, quarrelsome, backward and only interested in their own welfare and not in that of the village.

According to his account in one week he was able to recruit numerous members by explaining what the party would do for the country and for the village. By the end of a few months the party claimed approximately four hundred members. At the time of independence the branch's membership totalled approximately 1,800 with the majority living in Mto wa Mbu itself. This figure represented about 50 percent of the adult population at the time.

Although government administrative officers are present in the village the TANU chairman occupies the most important political position. Since 1955 there have been five such chairmen: a Kisii from Kenya; an Ngoni from Southern Tanzania, an Nguu from the coast; a Sandawe from the central area; and finally, a Zanaki from Western Tanzania. The chairman is elected by popular vote and ethnicity does not seem to have been a factor in selection since all of the chairmen were members of groups with a very small representation in the community except for the Nguu. However, they all have been Muslims, reflecting the previously mentioned religious bias in political choice. In remarking on this to the TANU chairman who was re-elected for a second five-year term in 1970, he resolutely claimed that the religious factor was mere coincidence, and indicated his disinterest in pursuing the topic. Indeed, although "tribalism" and its dangers were often discussed at political meetings, the subject of religion was never alluded to. The real potential for community schism along religious lines was obviously apparent to the political leaders and, therefore, never mentioned, even in disapproving terms, as opposed to "tribalism," which was a safe non-issue.

Organizationally, the party emerges at the lowest level, with a system of cells composed of ten houses in close proximity, which elects a leader from their number who is called *mzee wa nyumba kumi kumi* (the elder of ten houses). The community is also subdivided into various localities, with the cell leaders in the division choosing one of their members, as *mzee wa kijiji* (elder of the hamlet) to represent the area. All hamlet leaders are members of a Village Development Committee, which also includes representatives of the government agencies such as the health officer, the school headmaster, agricultural officer, the village executive officer and others, as well as officers of the TANU Youth League and the Union of Tanzanian Women.

This committee under the direction of the TANU chairman concerns itself with discussing community problems and projects and serves as a channel of communication through the cell leaders. Applications for land in the village are made through the village Development Committee as well as requests for irrigation rights. Community development schemes with compulsory attendance such as improvements of public buildings are also decided upon by the committee. In essence this organization and its decisions are of vital importance to every member of the village and all residents have a voice in it through their cell leaders.

The system of cell leaders although designed as a political mechanism serves many other purposes. For example, if a new individual moves into an area it is the responsibility of the cell leader to acquaint the new household of his rights and duties in terms of the use of the irrigation furrows. The cell leader is also responsible for maintaining peace and order in his jurisdiction and seeing that party policy and government ordinances are understood. Further, it is official policy that any disputes which take place within a cell such as those over land are first taken to the cell leader for resolution. If this fails the matter is then taken up by the *mzee wa kijiji* or the TANU chairman. Only if this fails are the disputants encouraged to take the matter to court. Further, the extremely important question of irrigation rights are dealt with through the party and the cell leaders. An individual can divert water to his fields only after requesting it through his cell leader who then transmits the petition to the *mzee wa kijiji* who oversees the entire program in the area and insures that rights to irrigation are equitable.

In discussing the introduction of this new system of authority to a traditional society it might be said that it was impinging upon or paralleling traditional political institutions. However, there are no detailed studies of this question and it is likely that party control and importance is minimal in this type of situation. By contrast, in Mto wa Mbu this system has taken hold immediately, and instead of competing with existing institutions, it has created a community-wide organization where none existed before.

Further, this cell system has incorporated many of the features of traditional societies which were readily accepted in the community. The cell leader resembles in his responsibilities a village headman and as a group they form a council of elders who serve to advise and guide the younger members of the village. This arrangement involves all the residents in a single set of relationships and creates a degree of unity and coherence which was almost entirely lacking in the pre-independence era. This offers an explanation for the party's rapid growth and importance in Mto wa Mbu. It also explains the feeling on the part of the inhabitants that since independence and due to TANU leadership the village is a much better place to live in than before.

VOLUNTARY ASSOCIATIONS

Social anthropologists who have carried out research in African cities south of the Sahara have pointed out and commented at length on the existence of voluntary associations. These associations serve a variety of purposes and are most often drawn along ethnic lines. Little (1965) in his study of these organizations in urban West Africa writes that:

> . . . the industrialized town presents a picture of conflicting as well as changing needs. It implies a social and psychological situation which might amount to Durkheim's notion of anomie were it not that voluntary

associations provide a link between the traditional and urban way of life . . . They build for the migrant a cultural bridge and in doing so they convey him from one kind of social universe to another (p. 87).

In another essay on the same subject he suggests that these associations composed of members of a single ethnic group provide defense and mutual aid in the hostile urban environment (Little 1967). Gordon Wilson (1961) has observed that in Mombasa there are over a hundred such groups and one composed entirely of Luo has attempted to prevent Luo women from becoming prostitutes or concubines to men of other groups. This supports the idea that a retention of ethnic solidarity in the urban environment is an important factor in these organizations. In addition, these associations may also have important economic functions and serve to protect their members in times of financial need by combining their resources.

The importance of this institution in urban areas and the lack of any such voluntary associations in Mto wa Mbu merits comment. Mto wa Mbu, like urban areas, is inhabited by representatives of numerous ethnic groups. On this basis alone it might be assumed that the community would be a fertile setting for the emergence of these associations. However, there are none in existence and even the Chagga who form such a close-knit group in the village have failed to organize themselves in this manner. This would suggest that such associations are primarily a characteristic feature of the urban scene and not a feature of the poly-ethnic agricultural setting.

The fact that Mto wa Mbu has an agricultural economic base in comparison to the wage labor one of the city greatly diminishes the possible value of these associations. A number of significant consequences can be cited. First, the migrant from the countryside to the city is culturally and socially ill equipped to handle basic problems such as finding a job, a place to live, where to buy food or even how much to pay for various items. Little (1965) in the above quotation has a valid point in stating that these associations provide a cultural bridge from one social universe to another. Contrastingly, the migrant who moves from one rural area to another is not faced with the traumatic situation which accompanies the rural to urban shift. He may have made a geographical move, but not a cultural one, and such problems that he does have are comparatively minor.

Secondly, the voluntary association in the city has an important economic function of serving to protect the urban dweller from the vicissitudes of wage labor and city living. Watson (1958) in his study of Mambwe has pointed out how the migrants view the rural area as the base providing true economic security in comparison to the city which offers short-term advantages. Since the migrant to Mto wa Mbu has retained his economic base in the land and agriculture, he is not subject to the same type of economic precariousness as the urban resident. As a result, financial aid associations become unnecessary since basic economic security is involved with the land and not primarily with the accumulation of cash.

The fact that agriculture in Mto wa Mbu is based on an irrigation system also has a negative effect on the emergence of ethnic associations whether of an economic or cultural type. With irrigation there is a necessity for large-scale cooperative labor among the inhabitants and this cooperation must cut across ethnic lines. In a democratic community this cooperation can only truly be sought on a voluntary basis even though there may be penalties for anti-social behavior. The development of ethnic associations in this situation would tend to emphasize divisions in the village where, as stated, economic success or failure is the result of cooperative effort. As a result, it is of vital importance that the residents identify their economic security with the community and not with any single group within it.

The manner in which any attempt to raise the specter of ethnicity in its negative connotation is met in Mto wa Mbu is illustrated in the following example. The fact that it pertains to a minor issue provides some indication of the reaction that formal ethnic associations would provoke.

At a general meeting it was announced that a new government policy required all able members of the village to participate in self-help community development projects. The TANU Chairman then suggested that the first project be the building of an outdoor kitchen for the village school where the few children boarders could prepare their meals.

This was generally agreed upon, but after a few minutes of

discussion it was pointed out by one of the residents that all of the children boarding at the school were Masai who did not live in the village. He wanted to know, therefore, if the Masai were also going to help in the construction, since it would be used primarily by their children. The TANU Chairman responded that he did not want to discuss who would use the kitchen or who should help build it, since the addition to the school would improve the village, which meant everyone. The dissenter then said that he was willing to help build the kitchen, even though his own children would not use it, but at least some Masai should be on hand to help out. The meeting came to a close with another statement by the Chairman on the importance of unity in the community and in Tanzania as a whole.

However, on the appointed day, the Chairman made an unsuccessful attempt to enlist a number of Masai for the project. Consequently, the issue of Masai cooperation was again raised at the building site by the same man. This time, rather than the ideology of unity being employed, the reaction was ridicule. While the complainer was commenting on the absence of Masai, and making generally unfavorable remarks about them, another interrupted to ask who and where the speaker was from. When the man answered that he was a Nyasa this was greeted by others with derision who pointed out that the Nyasa were not even from Tanzania so what was he doing here. Another worker who was also a government employee called him one of Banda's[2] men which was followed by more laughter. Shortly thereafter the conversation ended and no further complaints were heard about the Masai.

This incident serves to illustrate the sensitivity of the inhabitants to the subject of ethnicity. Although the majority of the people would have agreed that the Masai should have been participating in the project they did not take the side of the individual who raised the issue. Rather they chose to ridicule him into silence and side with the party and government officials on the issue of communal and national unity.

NOTES

1. To avoid confusion it should be noted that the original Nguvumali, a medicine man of great reputation on the Tanzanian coast and the subject of Peter Lienhardt's (1968) translation of the Swahili poem "Swifa ya Nguvumali,"had died by this time. It is possible that the Nguvumali of Mto wa Mbu was a student of the original or merely another medicine man with the same name. I am indebted to Dr. Lienhardt for pointing this out to me.
2. President Banda of Malawi was unpopular in Tanzania at the time because a few months previously he had made vague claims to some Tanzanian territory.

7

KINSHIP, MARRIAGE AND RELIGIOUS ADOPTION

In this chapter kinship, marriage patterns and conversion to Islam or Christianity are considered as basic social processes operative in the community. They are best seen as processes since except for the case of religion the result is not the formation of permanent groups. Rather, the outcome of the manipulation of kinship ties or marriage contracts is individualized personal networks. These networks in turn indicate the options available and decisions necessary for the residents in order to form new ties within the village or to continue involving themselves in existing ones extending to their original home.

For example, an inter-ethnic marriage to a co-villager can be seen as a decisive aspect in the process of establishing a new and qualitatively different set of social ties. The recognition and activation of all possible kinship ties or the decision to convert to one of the established religions can also be seen as an aspect of the same process. The individual is not presented merely with the opportunity to activate possible relationships, but with the choice of taking conscious steps to establish ties where none existed previously.

Having examined these processes, it will be possible, through the use of case studies, to define certain types of residents on the basis of their manipulation of these options, indicating an emphasis on participation in the social life of the community or another outside of it.

KINSHIP

Commenting on kinship in contemporary Africa, with reference to new forms of community organization, Southall (1961) has written that:

> . . . in the new situations the scope of kinship rights and duties has narrowed and become more uncertain and the body of kin included in them become reduced. In these situations the total contribution of kinship relations to the social structure is relatively less than in tribal subsistence communities, especially by comparison with relationships of more specialized economic, recreational, or other associational type (p. 31).

Southall's suggestion that it is misleading to attempt to define in structural terms the kinship system of an urban community composed of unrelated migrants from various ethnic groups holds for Mto wa Mbu. However, it should not be concluded that kinship itself diminishes in importance among the inhabitants of these communities. Fraenkel's study of urban Monrovia concludes that "The range of kinsfolk between whom obligations are accepted may in fact be larger in the urban community than in the traditional one" (1964:129).

This seeming contradiction about the contribution of kinship in the urban environment can be resolved by considering the composition of kinship groups in the rural societies, as opposed to urban centers. A frequent and basic characteristic of a kinship system in the former is that it provides the basis for the formation of corporate groups with a variety of functions. In urban areas corporate groups based on kinship do not emerge. These kin groups which are a feature of traditional rural societies become "destructured" in the city. What develops on the other hand is a situation where individuals recognize various types of relationships to other residents in the town. In the urban milieu the kinship network also has different functions in response to the demands of city life. It can be appreciated, therefore, that in both areas kinship is important and only the structure of the groups and their functions may vary.

Southall (1961) was referring to this lack of ideal structural patterns since he points out further on that:

. . . the range of kin provided for any town dweller is essentially incomplete. Many of the key positions in the kinship system to which he was reared remain vacant in the town. The collection of relatives with whom he is able to establish and maintain kinship in the urban context is miscellaneous and haphazard (p. 32).

Fraenkel on the other hand in stressing the importance of kinship in the urban area was concerned with the organization of these groups and the tendency of residents to manipulate their individual kinship networks in this situation.

In Mto wa Mbu the contribution of kinship to community structure is negligible since the principle of descent can not be employed in the formation of permanent groups. However, the importance of kinship networks remains significant. A distinctive feature of these networks is that they are not limited to the community. Although this varies to some degree, through these networks of kin the residents are able to retain their interest and actively participate on occasion in developments in their traditional homes. The ability or inclination to do so is influenced by such factors as physical distance from other kinsmen or the number of close relations living in Mto wa Mbu. Economic factors such as the retention of land or cattle at home or the possibility of inheriting these items from a close kinsman are significant reasons for maintaining these external ties. Residents often expressed their interest in kinship developments at home in exactly these terms. Some stated emphatically that if they were to inherit a good piece of land or especially cattle, they would return. Others expressed their relative indifference to their lack of property at home or hope of getting any and concentrated on improving their living conditions in Mto wa Mbu. The relationship between kinship and property, therefore, is crucial in maintaining important kinship ties over time and distance.

The variability in actual number of kinsmen which any one person has in the village is a further characteristic of kinship in this setting. As Southall (1961) indicates, in migrant settlements the kinship network is generally incomplete; but this statement glosses over the fact that there is a great deal of variation between cases. In Mto wa Mbu there are examples of some individuals who have only members of their own nuclear family living in the community while others are surrounded by numerous relatives. This

takes on significance when considering the effect it has on re-
stricting important social links within the physical boundaries
of the community in various ways.

The adult resident from a society with a traditional patrilineal
bias who is living in the village with his own father and siblings
as well as his father's brother and children of his father's brother
has the opportunity to remain in close contact with the most
important members of his immediate kinship network. This
localization of kinsmen reduces the number of important ties
existing outside of Mto wa Mbu. On the other hand, this same
situation diminishes the need to establish new ties on some basis
other than kinship within the village. Hence, in time of need or
crisis he is able and expected to call on his kinsmen rather than
others. The resident who has few if any relatives living close by
has a stronger need to retain existing ties to his original home.
At the same time he finds it to his advantage to contract non-
kinship bonds with other inhabitants of Mto wa Mbu.

Both Gutkind (1965) and Van Velsen (1961) have pointed
out in their studies of urban centers that the typical migrant
resident takes a keen interest in developments in the rural area.
The main reason for doing so is because the great majority of
these individuals left their immediate family at home which insures the maintenance of a "kin-based network" (Gutkind 1965:
54). The average adult male in Mto wa Mbu differs in this respect
since his wife and children are with him. However, he presents
a similar picture to the urban dweller since in most cases other
members of his kinship network remain in his original home.
The number and type of kinsmen within the village, therefore,
partially determine the kinds of new relationships which will be
forged in Mto wa Mbu.

Turning to the actual figures (table 5) it was found that by
1969 approximately two-thirds (67.5 percent) of the heads of
households had some sort of kin or affine living in the village.
Among those surveyed slightly more than half (54.9 percent) were
found to have consanguineal kin or both consanguineal kin and
affines, excluding members of the nuclear family, in residence.
Only a few (12.6 percent) had affinal but no consanguineal relations. This left a minority of less than one-third (32.4 percent)
with neither kin nor affines. As is to be expected, the number and

type of kinsmen varied greatly. This indicates that for at least two-thirds of the settlers kinship is a potentially important aspect of inter-personal relations. Thus, village social organization can not be seen as being composed of discrete nuclear family units, but rather to some extent as units tied into a larger network based on various types of kinship and affinal links.

Table 5. Heads of Household with Kinsmen and Affines in Residence

Heads of Household	% With Kin or Kin and Affines	% With Affines Only	% Without Kin or Affines
On Arrival	40.5	9.0	50.4
By 1969	54.9	12.6	32.4

Source: 1969 Field Survey of Households (N = 111 heads of household).

One of the important functions of kinship in Mto wa Mbu, as in urban centers, is the role kinsmen play in introducing a new member to the community. In the city it is generally a kinsman or at least a close friend from the same rural area who introduces the new migrant to the differences in urban living and helps in solving some of the basic problems. The same applies in Mto wa Mbu where a kinsman will play an important part in helping to establish a recent arrival by providing him with a place to live, advice on where to purchase and how to apply for land. It was not surprising to find, therefore, that almost one-half of the migrants had some sort of relative already in residence at the time of arrival. As can be assumed from the previously cited figures, the great majority were consanguines (40.5 percent). When these figures were looked at in relation to year of arrival (table 6) it was found that over half (55.3 percent) of those arriving between 1930 and 1949 had some sort of kin or affine already there; between 1950 and 1959 only slight more than a third (37.5 percent) and between 1960 and 1969 one-half (51 percent). The decrease between 1950 and 1959 is a result of the arrival of the Chagga in large numbers during this period. Since a portion of these migrants were the first of their kind to

Table 6. Heads of Household with/without Kinsmen and Affines in Residence
By Year of Arrival

Year of Arrival	Number Heads of Household	Percentage With Kin &/or Affines	Percentage Without Kin or Affines
1930-1949	38	55.3	44.7
1950-1959	24	37.5	62.5
1960-1969	49	51.0	48.9
Total	111	49.5	50.5

Source: 1969 Field Survey of Households (N = 111 heads of household).

settle in Mto wa Mbu they naturally lacked kinsmen.

As a result of the incompleteness of the kinship network of any individual it follows then that the types of kinsmen involved in any one case will also vary. A resident might have his mother's brother living in the vicinity, but not his father's brother or neither of these two while the children of his mother's sister may have settled there. The result is that, as Southall (1961:34) has suggested, traditional specific categories are replaced by a general class of individuals who are referred to simply as kinsmen. In Swahili the word *jamaa* is used which adequately reflects the irregularity of kin groups in this setting.

Jamaa can be used in Swahili to refer to a collection of people for any purpose. However, when a resident of Mto wa Mbu uses the term it refers specifically to those he considers kinsmen, a group including all those in the community who he could possibly claim some connection to either through descent or marriage. The term is translated by Prins (1967:81) as a kindred since it does not refer to a specific enduring group, but rather to a collection of individuals around a specific focus. Since the point of reference is a living individual and not an ancestor the composition of this grouping varies depending upon the ego involved.

At certain times an individual's *jamaa* also includes non-kinsmen such as friends and neighbors. When the events of a wedding which was to take place on the next day were being described to me, I was told that the groom and his *jamaa* would walk together to the bride's house to meet with her *jamaa*. I assumed that this would involve only a small number of people, but upon arrival I found at least fifty people waiting to escort the groom. It was explained that they were his *jamaa*, but in reality only a few were actual kinsmen.

A *jamaa* therefore is a "quasi-group" (Boissevain 1968) loosely tied together by various kinds of structural principles but having an ideology based on kinship. An individual's *jamaa* comes together only on ritual occasions as expressions of emotional solidarity and has no other corporate functions. More important than the group itself are the dyadic relationships contained within it.

The vernacular of kinship, therefore, is often employed to establish relationships where no true genealogical or affinal tie exists. It is not uncommon to hear unrelated people greeting each other with the use of kinship terms. One of the most common of these is *shemeji* which with a male ego means brother or sister-in-law, but is frequently used among individuals of the same generation to refer to someone who has married a member of his extended *jamaa*. A man will call a woman who has married a kinsman of the same generation no matter what the degree of relationship his *shemeji* and she will respond in kind. It might also be used to refer to someone who has married a close friend, a neighbor or even just a member of the same ethnic group. In some cases, the relationship is an extremely casual one and never goes beyond the use of the term. In others though it takes on all the characteristics of a close bond.

Other examples of such pseudo-kinship relationships could be mentioned, but as a rule these bonds are only established among individuals on the basis of fictional affinal links and not con-sanguineal ones. For example, two men who worked together and lived next to each other called each other's wife *shemeji*. The women referred to each other as *wifi* (sister-in-law), but the males never addressed each other as *kaka* (brother). The men themselves preferred to express their relationship in terms of *urafiki* (friendship) which carries with it fewer responsibilities than that of a close kinship tie.

This brief discussion of the manner in which kinship is employed illustrates its use as a means of establishing links with other residents. It is a readily available mechanism that can be seized upon by any new arrival in the process of establishing his social presence or by an established resident in expanding his social field. Kinsman is an ill defined social category since all sorts of relationships are recognized and activated whereas this might not be the case in a traditional setting.

The vagueness and manipulation of kinship ties in Mto wa Mbu is not an aspect of social change among formerly patrilineal or matrilineal people who have now come to trace descent cognatically. Rather it reflects a specific situation in which it is expedient for the individual to recognize different kinship categories than he might at home. Not only are there various possibilities to manipulate relationships, but even the concept of kinship itself is manipulated to establish ties where none existed before.

A final quality of kinship in the community is the clear-cut bias amongst all of the residents toward patrilineality in many respects. For example, regardless of the traditional means of tracing descent, an individual will claim the same ethnic identity as his father. In a discussion with a young man whose mother was a Nyamwezi and father an Iramba he stated that he was an Iramba. When I pointed out that the Iramba took the mother's clan and not the father's, and on this basis he was a Nyamwezi he replied that maybe this was so, but in Mto wa Mbu he was an Iramba. This was interesting since his father left his mother when he was a child and the youth and his mother were living with her parents. All the other members of the household claimed to be Nyamwezi, but they all considered the boy to be an Iramba.

This discussion of kinship is not complete without returning again to the subject of the Swahili culture and language. The Swahili kinship system is cognatic and corresponds in classical form only to the traditional means of ordering relationships among certain groups living on the East African coast. Finer terminological distinctions which may be used by some coastal speakers, such as the differentiation among father's sister's children and mother's brother's children are not made in Mto wa Mbu where they are more simply classed together by the use of a single term.

Although groups are formed on the basis of the principle of cognatic descent, Wijeyewardene (1959a) states that the Swahili system is basically an ordering of relationships between individuals rather than groups. Terminologically it is a classificatory system with a minimum of categories. The biological father and his brothers are grouped together and are called *baba* (father) while the mother and her sisters are all called *mama* (mother). However, it is possible to distinguish the biological father *(baba mzazi)* and mother *(mama mzazi)*. It is also possible to distinguish between the father's elder and younger brothers *(baba mkubwa, baba mdogo)* and the same is possible for the mother's sisters *(mama mkubwa, mama mdogo)*. The term *ndugu* is used for siblings and children of classificatory parents. The father's sisters are distinguished by the term *shangazi* while the mother's brothers are referred to as *mjomba*. Their children are called *binamu*. In addition to distinguishing between parallel and cross cousins the latter are among coastal groups preferred marriage partners and the former prohibited (Lienhard 1968). There was no indication of this type of preference among the residents of Mto wa Mbu many of whom would consider this type of union incestuous.

As a cognatic system characterized by a classificatory terminology it could not possibly reflect the traditional ordering and labelling of relationships for all of the residents of Mto wa Mbu. For example, at home an individual employing traditional terminology and categories of kinsmen of a unilateral system would distinguish between the children of his mother's siblings and father's siblings. The one group of individuals are members of his own lineage and clan while the others are not. However, the same person in Mto wa Mbu by using *Kiswahili* terms with its broad classificatory labels recognizes all of these individuals whether related matrilaterally or patrilaterally as either *ndugu* or *binamu*. In effect, he is able to cast the net of kinship over a wider group of people. The Swahili system and terminology, therefore, is particularly adaptable to the social situation in Mto wa Mbu where it may be of interest to recognize all possible relationships whether matrilateral or patrilateral and treat them as an undifferentiated class. The use of Swahili terminology facilitates this process since it allows the inhabitants to recognize a greater number of kinsmen of the same type and degree.

MARRIAGE PATTERNS

Marriage in Mto wa Mbu because of its predominantly Muslim-Christian character abides by religious and civil regulations as well as traditional marriage customs of a general nature. In all cases where the marriage has been solemnized by a civil, religious or traditional ceremony a bride price *(mahari)* is paid to the girl's father or her closest patrilineal kinsman. In those instances where marriages have been contracted between villagers the *mahari* involves a cash payment and usually also includes some small gifts such as cloth for the bride as well as her mother. Among the Muslims if the girl is found to be a virgin the groom also gives the bride's mother a cash gift in recognition of the mother's diligence in raising the child. The amount of the *mahari* is agreed upon in advance, but on the day of the ceremony or shortly before, the details of the transaction such as the amount already paid and that remaining are officially recorded with the village administrative officer responsible for registering marriages. This is done by the groom, bride's father and witnesses for each party to insure that misunderstandings are kept to a minimum. All further payments after marriage also take place in the presence of witnesses. For those residents who return home to choose a wife, the bride price usually includes more traditional items such as cattle, goats or beer; but since these are not easily obtainable in Mto wa Mbu the medium of exchange is always cash, the sum varying between 200 and 800 shillings.

The bride price agreed upon by the two parties involves consideration of the age and reputation of the intended bride as well as that of her family. A higher figure would be offered for a young asssumed virgin who has been under the constant supervision of her family than for an older girl who is frequently in the village on her own. Brandel (1959) has suggested that in the city African girls consider the marriage payment an indication of their social worth. However, it is not only the reputation and status of the bride and her family which is taken into consideration in settling the bride price, but also that of the groom. In addition to his prestige and economic position in the community the religious reputation of the intended groom is of great importance, particularly among the Muslims. Consequently, a devout Muslim, especially one whose religious education has reached the point where he has gained the title of *mwalimu*, normally is able to offer less to secure a highly respected bride than another member of the community. The reasoning behind such a decision is that whatever the bride's family loses economically in such an arrangement is more than compensated for by their prestige gain.

In addition to these unions, some couples live together without going through the formality of a legal wedding. Only a few cases were noted, since the great majority of the population abides by Muslim or Christian custom. The normal procedure when there is no official ceremony is for the male to begin paying the bride price to the wife's parents if a child has been born. The sum is usually less than is the case in a formal union. In one instance the husband gave the money directly to his wife, since she had no relatives in the community.

A quantitative description of marriage patterns in Mto wa Mbu is also important because it provides an opportunity to assess the relevance of ethnicity at the level of interpersonal relations. Choosing a spouse presents the resident with a situation of alternative possibilities, since a marriage partner may be selected from one's own or another ethnic group. The assumption is that the kind of marriages which are contracted is a crucial factor in the emergence of a community with internal cross-cutting ties and with a de-emphasis on ethnic exclusiveness. Marriage across ethnic boundaries may also be interpreted as an expression of attachment and adjustment to the poly-ethnic setting. Marriages with established residents create affinal ties within the community and provide ready access to a network of individuals in time of need. At the same time, these inter-ethnic unions reflect the decision not to create new ties to traditional homelands. Therefore, the extent of mixed-ethnic marriages within a community is an indicator of individuals' commitment to long-term residence as well as a predictor of community integration.

Duration of village residence and the retention of economic interests in a traditional home may also affect the likelihood of inter-ethnic marriage since they are additional indicators of community involvement. Whether or not individuals marrying for the first time choose a co-ethnic partner is another significant factor. Individuals marrying for second and subsequent times in

Mto wa Mbu are likely to have a history of migration and thus probably are more inclined than recent arrivals to marry inter-ethnically.

Naturally, the composition of the community population, especially the sex ratio and age structure of specific ethnic representations will affect the opportunities for selecting co-ethnic mariage partners within the village. However, since most residents have easy access to their traditional homes, the opportunity exists, and is utilized, for arranging a marriage with a co-ethnic non-resident. Thus, the market of co-ethnics is relatively un-restricted.

The following analysis is based on a survey of marital histories (Arens and Arens 1978). Data were collected by systematic sampling of the male heads of household (N = 223) of every fifth dwelling which produced 235 extant marriages. Each respondent was asked to provide information on his ethnic background, religion, year of arrival to the community, time and place of marriage and wife's or wives' social background. The ethnic and religious composition of the sample was similar to that reported in the 1957 and 1967 censuses. Muslims accounted for 54 percent of the sample, Christians 38 percent and traditionalists 8 percent. Although many of the respondents (40 percent) had more than one marriage at some time, the great majority (82 percent) had only one wife at the time of the survey. The Muslim men tended to marry more often than the Christians; however, this indicated divorce and remarriage rather than polygyny. Whether or not a man had more than one wife at the same time was a function of economic arrangements rather than religious persuasion.

As mentioned, each respondent was asked to give his own and his wife's ethnic label. However, it cannot be assumed *ipso facto* that if these were different then the marriage was mixed in the sense of significant cultural differences between the partners. Such labels may be artificial since often more similarities than variations exist between two supposed "tribes." In Tanzania, at least the major dividing line between two groups may actually be the district boundary drawn a few decades ago by the colonial administration. Therefore, in attempting to determine if there was a degree of inter-ethnic marriage worthy of consideration, the sample was initially classified according to Murdock's (1959) "ethnic clusters" which include a number of different groups. These clusters are based on similarities in economic and subsistence patterns, social organization, language, customs and geographical proximity.

When the sample of extant marriages (N = 235) which included individuals representing fifty-five stated ethnic categories is reclassified into sixteen clusters, not surprisingly, the number of mixed marriages is reduced. Yet even this system which allows for greater heterogeneity within groups yields 26 percent mixed unions. If only extant marriages entered into after arrival (N = 116) are taken into account, the proportion of mixed unions is 34 percent. Thus, community members of varied cultural backgrounds were indeed entering into legal unions.

Table 7 shows that when the stated ethnic labels of the respondents were accepted as given, 38 percent of the marriages (235) were inter-ethnic. Considering the number which post-date arrival to the community (116), 47 percent were inter-ethnic while only 29 percent of the marriages which pre-date settlement (119) were of this type. This comparison yields a differential of 18 percentage points. Finally, 70 percent of the marriages which were forged after arrival and actually took place in Mto wa Mbu (44) were between spouses with different ethnic backgrounds. These rates are high in comparison to those reported for urban African centers.

Table 7. Percentage of Mixed-Ethnic Marriages by Time of Marriage

| | Time of Marriage | | |
	Before Arrival in Mto wa Mbu % #	After Arrival in Mto wa Mbu % #+	Total
Mixed-Ethnic Marriages	29 (119)	47 (116)	38 (235)

Residence in Mto wa Mbu at the time of marriage clearly increases the likelihood of choosing a spouse from another ethnic category. Table 8 shows no difference, however, between the proportion of inter-ethnic marriages contracted after 0-9 years residence (45 percent) and unions formed after 10 or more years

Table 8. Percentage of Mixed-Ethnic Marriages Contracted After Arrival
by Type of Marriage and Length of Residence when Married, and by
Economic Interest in Traditional Homeland

| | *Type of Marriage* | | |
	First Marriages % #	Second and Subsequent Marriages % #	Total % #
Length of Residence			
0-9 Years	21 (33)	68 (34)	45 (67)
10 Yrs. & Over	47 (19)	50 (30)	49 (49)
Total	31 (52)	59 (64)	(116)
Economic Interest			
Yes	6 (16)	55 (29)	38 (45)
No	42 (36)	63 (35)	52 (71)

Source: 1969 Field Survey of Marriage Patterns (N = 223 males heads
of household).

(49 percent). Nevertheless, before concluding that length of residence has no effect on intermarriage, marital histories must be taken into account. First marriages are 28 percentage points less likely to be inter-ethnic than others (respectively, 31 percent and 59 percent). Thus individuals who have never married seem constrained by ethnic considerations in choosing a spouse. Newer residents marrying for the first time have a strikingly low rate (21 percent) of mixed-ethnic marriages. Although the implications are only suggestive, it is possible that these men are hesitant to intermarry because as relative newcomers they are undecided as to whether or not they will return to their traditional homes. It is not clear why new residents who have been married previously choose inter-ethnic partners even more often than older residents contracting the same type of marriage. However, one relevant factor is certainly that new residents to the community have much to gain by opting for a co-resident as a spouse since such an alliance would facilitate settlement in the community.

Similarly, table 8 indicates that men who retain an economic interest in their homeland were 36 percentage points less likely to contract mixed-ethnic marriages after arrival to Mto wa Mbu than those who had severed such ties. For subsequent unions this differential decreases to 8 percentage points.

In sum, initial marriages tend to be within ethnic boundaries. However, established male residents marrying for the first time have more mixed marriages than new arrivals. In the same vein, men who do not have economic interests in their traditional homes contract more mixed unions than men who retain these ties. In contrast, subsequent marriages in general are likely to be mixed ethnically. In these cases, duration of residence and economic ties to a traditional home do not have the same effect.

Religion also assumes an importance in the choice of a marriage partner. For the Christian and Muslim population approximately 95 percent of the unions are between partners of like religious persuasion. Table 9 shows that the Muslims are almost twice as likely as Christians to have inter-ethnic marriages (respectively, 47 percent and 25 percent). Initially, the pattern appears to support the prevailing though often unsubstantiated opinion that Islam is more effective than Christianity in diminishing the relevance of ethnicity among its adherents (Arens 1975b). However, a closer examination shows that both Muslims and Christians are more likely to have inter-ethnic marriages if the arrangement was made after residence in Mto wa Mbu. Comparison of inter-ethnic marriages of Muslims and Christians which pre-date arrival yields a differential of 21 percentage points while the differential between the two for marriages after arrival decreases slightly to 15 percentage points.

Table 9. Percentage of Mixed-Ethnic Marriages by Religion of Men and by Time of Arrival

| | Religion | |
| | Christian | Muslim |
Time of Arrival	% #	% #
Before Arrival	18 (54)	39 (51)
After Arrival	36 (33)	51 (78)
Total	25 (87)	47 (129)

The analysis suggests that number of years in the village has an additional positive influence on choosing a spouse from a different ethnic group for first marriages. This may account for the higher percentage of mixed marriages among the Muslims who are the majority of established residents. However, the sample is too small to simultaneously examine the three variables: religion, type of marriage and length of residence.

When the effects of type of marriage and religion are examined, analysis is still rather speculative since there are too few cases within these categories. However, table 10 reveals consistent trends. If it is not the initial one, inter-ethnic marriage increases and a striking pattern emerges. The proportion of Christian inter-ethnic first marriages is 11 percent and this increases to 67 percent for subsequent ones. The differential between Muslims and Christians on this score is 30 percentage points. For subsequent marriages there is a much smaller differential, 8 percentage points. Perhaps even more interesting, Christians have a slightly higher proportion of mixed ethnic second and subsequent marriages than Muslims.

Table 10. Percentage of Mixed-Ethnic Marriages Contracted after Arrival by Religion of Men and Type of Marriage

| | Religion | |
| | Christian | Muslim |
Type of Marriage	% #	% #
First Marriage	11 (18)	41 (32)
Second and Subsequent Marr.	67 (15)	59 (46)

Hence, although Muslims tend to choose a spouse from another ethnic group more often than Christians regardless of time of marriage, establishment of residence in Mto wa Mbu has the overall effect of minimizing differences between the two groups. Further, Christians and Muslims who are not marrying for the first time have similar mixed-ethnic rates.

ETHNICITY AND MARRIAGE IN URBAN CENTERS

In order to gauge the comparative character of marriage patterns in Mto wa Mbu, every effort was made to gather representative statistical information on inter-ethnic marriages for urbanized areas of Sub-Saharan Africa. However, comparison of marriage patterns in Mto wa Mbu with those in urban centers is not as enlightening as initially hoped. In many cases, data on inter-ethnic marriages were simply not collected, and in others sampling procedures do not allow for generalization.

Table 11 provides data on the urban communities discussed. In brief, the inter-ethnic marriage rates for Mto wa Mbu exceed, by a minimum of 20 percentage points, those reported for Stanleyville (Pons 1969:96); Jinja (Sofer and Sofer 1955:78); Lagos (Marris 1961:160); Kampala (Parkin 1969:97-104); and Mulago, a suburb of Kampala (Southall and Gutkind 1957:170-1).

Mitchell's (1957:16) survey in Luanshya, a Zambian mining town (N = 183 registered marriages) resulted in 59 percent "inter-tribal" links, but these figures only include those marriages which took place in the community. The rate for Mto wa Mbu with this stricture is 70 percent. In addition, Mitchell (1957:5) suggests that there was a greater likelihood that "inter-tribal" rather than homogeneous unions would be officially recorded since the latter were recognized as valid by the colonial regime on the basis of the couple's customary law, while the former were not. Thus, there would be a greater stimulus for those involved to officially record this kind of marriage. Mitchell also re-analyzed the data in terms of seven ethnic clusters, and in doing so the inter-ethnic rate declined to 28 percent. However, as just noted his sample is too biased in favor of what he refers to as "inter-tribal cases" to conclude that this proportion was a good estimate of the degree of mixed marriages.

Wilson (1942:41) reports 30 percent inter-ethnic marriages in Broken Hill (Kabwe), Zambia, another miners' compound on the Copperbelt. However, not all of these were socially or apparently legally recognized. His discussion also suggests that he included as a marriage temporary liaisons between a short-term male migrant and a more permanent female resident. This procedure would result in an increase in inter-ethnic unions.

Banton's (1957:199-201) research in Freetown, Sierra Leone uncovers a relatively high proportion, 36 percent, of inter-ethnic marriages. However, his rates are derived from the "tribal designation" of the parents which were recorded on the birth certificates

Table 11. Selected African Urban Communities: Mixed-Ethnic Marriages
and Residential Stability[1]

Community	% Mixed-ethnic Marr.	(Sample Size)	Differ-ential[2]	% Pop. in residence less than 10-11 yrs.	(Sample Size)
Mto wa Mbu	38* 70† 26**	(235 extant marr.)	— — —	44	(223 adult males)
Stanleyville (Kisangani)	18* 21†	(719 extant marr.)	+20 +49	68	(1680 adult males)
Jinja	8*	(367 extant marr.)	+30	83	(1099 adult males inc. 1.4% visitors)
				80	(512 adult females inc. 2.5% visitors)
Rehousing estate in Lagos	13*	(55 extant marr.)	+25	17	(63 adults)
Central Lagos householders	2*	(124 extant marr.)	+36	11	(110 householders)
Kampala (Naguru & Nakawa Estate)	17*	(160 extant marr.)	+21	96	(645 Naguru house-hold heads inc. 2% unknown)
				97	(823 Nakawa house-hold heads inc. 2% unknown)
Mulago (Kampala)	18*	(1339 total pop.)	+20	78	(630 adult males)
Luanshya	59† 28**	(183 regis-tered marr.)	+11 -2	62 78	(182 bridegrooms) (182 brides)
Broken Hill (Kabwe)	30*	(based on pop. of 3500)	+8	Not Available	
Freetown	36*	(3071 registered births)	+2	53	(268 male heads of household)
Rooiyard (Johannesburg)	55*	(100 families total pop. 80 recognized marr.)	-7	Not Applicable	

[1] Most percentages were calculated from data supplied in the various ethnographies.
[2] Differential is calculated by subtracting percentage of mixed-ethnic marriages in selected urban community from comparable percentage in Mto wa Mbu.
* Percentage of mixed-ethnic marriages out of total extant marriages.
† Percentage of mixed-ethnic marriages out of extant marriages which took place in community itself.
** Percentage of mixed-ethnic marriages out of total extant marriages categorized by ethnic clusters.

Sources: Pons 1969; Sofer and Sofer 1955; Marris 1961; Parkin 1969; Southall and Gutkind 1957; Mitchell 1957; Wilson 1942; Banton 1957; Hellmann 1948.

of the public registry in Freetown (N = 3071) births). He points out (Banton, 1957:199) that the high inter-ethnic figure is possibly the result of women involved in a mixed marriage remaining in the city to give birth while those married to men of the same ethnic group in more instances return home for the event. In addition, a high proportion of his cases were between individuals with what Banton calls strong ties of similarity, so it is difficult to determine if these involved spouses with significantly different cultural backgrounds.

Finally, Hellmann (1948:13) recorded eighty recognized marriages, i.e., religious, civil and Native Customary Union, in Rooiyard, a "slumyard" in Johannesburg (N = total population 235 adults, 141 children). She found that 55 percent (N = 80) were inter-ethnic which is the single estimate exceeding that for Mto wa Mbu.

In sum, on the basis of available statistics the rate of inter-ethnic marriages in the rural poly-ethnic community of Mto wa Mbu is generally equal to, and in most cases higher than, that reported for urban Sub-Saharan Africa.

The analysis of marriage patterns in Mto wa Mbu shows that individuals who have migration histories or who have severed ties with traditional homes and settled in Mto wa Mbu on a permanent basis are likely to contract mixed marriages. This suggests the hypothesis that residentially stable and ethnically heterogeneous communities whether rural or urban will have high mixed-ethnic marriage rates. Table 11 indicates that Stanleyville, Jinja, Kampala, Mulago and the Zambian mining centers have relatively circulating populations and low rates of inter-ethnic marriage. Freetown and Mto wa Mbu, on the other hand, have residentially stable populations with smaller proportions of newer migrants in their adult population and higher rates of inter-ethnic marriages. Lagos does not fit the model since the population is relatively stable and the rate of inter-ethnic marriage is low. This pattern suggests that as more comparative data are collected, we may fruitfully evaluate the relation between the residential stability of communities and the degree of inter-ethnic marriage.

The preceding discussion of ethnic relations in Mto wa Mbu, seen from the perspective of kinship and marriage, lends itself to the following conclusions. There is little difference in the expression of kinship in this rural community to that which has been described for urban Africa. On this issue, it is not possible to posit a difference between heterogeneous rural and urban communities as a linear model would suggest. The immigration factor which is the crucial element results in similar arrangements in either type of settlement.

Migrants to a rural or uban poly-ethnic center activate all possible kin ties in the process of accommodation to the novel setting, and the groups which emerge on this basis are ego-centered and amorphous in character. Although it is ideally possible to argue that individuals have a choice in recognizing kinship ties, in reality there is severe pressure towards maintaining these relationships because they pre-date settlement in Mto wa Mbu. Naturally, one cannot choose consanguineal kin so that in effect the outcome is somewhat predetermined. An individual who failed to recognize and act on such ties obviously would be subjected to social disapproval. Although this may circumscribe some relationships within ethnic boundaries, it is kinship, not common ethnicity, which is being emphasized.

The choice of a marriage partner, though, is not as strongly predetermined since the individual has real alternatives in this matter. The data indicate that the choice of a spouse from the same ethnic background as an expression of the importance of ethnicity is certainly not always a primary consideration for the inhabitants of Mto wa Mbu. Establishing residence in this rural community diminishes the significance of the ethnic factor at the interpersonal level of mate selection. Common ethnicity is particularly unimportant if the marriage is not one's first, length of residence in Mto wa Mbu is long term, and economic ties with traditional homes have been severed. This is at variance with comparable reports on urban centers where to a greater extent residents choose a partner from the same ethnic category. This is also in opposition to the expectations of a rural-urban dichotomy which associates urbanism with a greater tolerance of social differences such as disparate ethnic backgrounds.

An examination of marriage patterns indicates some differences between the Christian and Muslim populations since the latter establish more inter-ethnic unions. However, an argument which assumes an inherent ideological ability of Islam as opposed to

Christianity to subsume the relevance of ethnic differences in the choice of a spouse was shown to be false when other factors, such as marital histories, were considered. Since Muslims are older participants in the migration stream in eastern Africa, and the majority of the earliest settlers in Mto wa Mbu were Muslims, this seems to affect their proclivity to choose a spouse from a different ethnic category. Therefore, as the number of Christians who migrate increases and ties to traditional homes are weakened, religious differentials in the inclination to devaluate ethnicity might well vanish.

The preceding analysis and discussion strongly suggests that facile assumptions about the nature of urban and rural Africa in terms of a folk-urban continuum are untenable, especially in light of the data on marriage patterns. Although social anthropologists have been long aware of the theoretical shortcomings of this concept, it nonetheless often influences their general thinking about contemporary social trends on the continent. As was the case with the role of ethnicity in the poly-ethnic rural setting, a thoughtful analysis requires the dismissal of existing preconceived notions in favor of flexible consideration of the ethnographic material.

THE RELIGIOUS PROCESS

Religion was examined earlier as an aspect of community structure and is returned to again for consideration from the standpoint of the processes involved in the formation of these groups. The question here becomes one of analyzing a new community member's means, motivations and decisions in choosing to accept one of the established religions. In the event that the migrant is already a member of an established religion upon arrival, what does this mean in terms of his acceptance by other members of the village?

Interestingly enough Max Weber's (1958) "The Protestant Sects and the Spirit of Capitalism" which sought to analyze the significance of religion in American frontier communities provides a comparative framework for the consideration of the same question in an African frontier village. Weber saw sect affiliation in early twentieth-century America as an indication of an individual's status in his community since it meant an individual had met certain standards of behavior and that his character and trustworthiness were beyond reproach by other members of the same group. Membership insured the economic and social support of the entire group while also providing a basic means of social identification.

In the essay Weber also deals with conversion and its meaning in relation to commerce. Conversion was prevalent in new growing settlements of early America and according to Weber it could be seen as the process by which an individual enters into the social and economic affairs of the community. He wrote:

> Admission to the congregation is recognized as an absolute guarantee of the moral qualities of a gentleman, especially of those qualities required in business matters. Baptism secures to the individual the deposits of the whole region and unlimited credit without any competition. He is a 'made man' . . . When a sect member moved to a different place, or if he were a travelling salesman, he carried the certificate of the congregation with him; and thereby he found not only easy contact with sect members but, above all, he found credit everywhere (p. 305).

Although Weber was dealing with "sects" in a capitalist economic system, these ideas are also applicable to an agricultural community where new settlers arrive regularly. The individual who comes to settle in the community and makes known the fact that he is a Muslim or a Christian is stating to established residents of the same faith that he shares with them a common set of beliefs and values. In a more mundane sphere it proposes that he be accepted on this basis and that aid in establishing himself in the community can be requested and granted on the grounds of a shared religious association.

On the other hand, the individual who appears on the scene professing no religious belief other than that of his ancestors is an unknown quality. He can make no claim for acceptance or aid on a religious basis, and has to fall back on ties of ethnic affiliation or kinship if possible. On the other hand, after a period of time he could choose to convert to Islam as a means of further acceptance. Since Mto wa Mbu was in the early days overwhelmingly Muslim, conversion was a frequent occurrence and provided the means for the creation of numerous ties. In many cases, it also facilitated marriage to the daughter of another resident and thereby created another set of ties binding him closer to existing social networks. Especially in the case of conversion, the benefits of belonging to one of the existing religious communities become quite apparent and worth consideration on non-theological grounds. In many ways religious affiliation is the most important factor in interpersonal relations. As a means of inter-action it defines a person in terms of a reliable set of ethical standards. On the other hand, ethnic affiliation alone may denote only unfamiliar beliefs and customs.

As indicated, during the community's first few decades it was more Muslim in character than at present, since many of the earliest settlers came from Muslim areas of Tanzania, while Chris-tian missions were not opened until a rather late date. Conse-quently, many of the other early migrants who were traditionalists were steadily converted to Islam by Muslims in residence.

In the normal course of events, a migrant who had no religious preference eventually established a relationship with a Muslim. During the course of time, the Muslim would initiate a discussion on Islam and if interest was shown, the dialogue continued along these lines until the non-believer indicated an interest in becoming a Muslim and requested further religious instruction. This responsi-bility was undertaken by the man's sponsor, who then informed him of the basic tenets of the religion. Eventually the neophyte would be initiated by the spiritual advisor into the fellowship of Islam.

This ceremony of incorporation established a bond between the two, encompassed by the ideology of a paternity. Only if asked directly will it become apparent that the man whom an individual calls father is not his genitor, but rather his *baba ya dini* (religious father) and that he is the man's *mtoto wa dini* (religious child). Many of the obligations attached to this bond are also similar to the biological one. For example, the father is able to call upon his son for small favors or services and in turn accepts a similar responsibility. As a further consequence, if the son wishes to marry, he must first seek his father's permission, but the latter must contribute to the bride price and in some cases accept full economic responsibility. This is not the usual procedure, since an individual who wishes to marry is expected to contribute as much as he is able from his own resources. However, in the past, a young man living far from his home and kin, and having little money, often would have to rely completely on his religious father in order to marry.

The reverse of this arrangement also holds true when a man serves as a sponsor and becomes the father of a female convert, since with her marriage he is entitled to a token portion of the bride price. However, the relationship between a daughter and her religious father is usually not as vital as that between two males. The females are usually living in the village with other relatives, and, consequently, the dependence on her religious father is not as crucial. In contrast, many of the males in the early days migrated by themselves and in the beginning had no kinsmen in the community, so that their relationship with their sponsor was the most important one.

The importance of this arrangement is further highlighted by the fact that this relationship, although contracted by two persons, extends along the kinship network of the sponsor. In practice it involves a tie between a single individual, the convert, and a group which includes the sponsor and his close kinsmen. Following Kiswahili kinship terminology, and assuming that they are all Muslims, the convert also refers to his new father's brothers as father and his sponsor's wife and her sisters as mother. Correspondingly, he calls the children of his sponsor his brothers and sisters. In the cases where the father has formally introduced more than one son or daughter to Islam they also call each other brother and sister.

Ideally, in all cases the individuals accept the same social obligations as if a biological relationship existed. Unfortunately, I did not determine if an incest restriction prohibited marriage between the convert and members of the opposite sex of his sponsor's family. Ishige (1969) who mentions conversion briefly has stated that a convert took his sponsor's daughter as his second wife. However, Guillotte (1970) carrying out research in a similar village in Northern Tanzania states this would not be possible according to his informants. My own impression from general discussions is that marriage between a convert and other members of this group would be prohibited.

The strength and importance of this religious tie may vary from one relationship to another, but the bond between the father and son is the strongest and most responsible. Nevertheless, it may be refuted if one of the parties does not meet his responsibilities or if the convert fails to follow the tenets of Islam to the satisfaction of his sponsor.

From a sociological standpoint the implications of this practice are profound. First, it creates special and close ties between individuals and groups on the basis of religion where none existed before. Further, an individual who entered the community where he had no ties is drawn into an already existing kinship network and a set of new relationships by his acceptance of Islam. This was a fairly common occurrence in the early days of the community when many migrants arrived as complete strangers.

Secondly, since this type of arrangement was frequently contracted by individuals from different backgrounds it served to create a link across ethnic lines. In addition to having a "father" of a different ethnic group, an individual may also establish ties with fellow converts of the same sponsor from a number of other groups. In short, this practice has served and continues to serve as a mechanism for preventing the emergence of ethnic groups within the community and creates vertical relationships between individuals which stretch throughout the village.

An example serves to clarify exactly what this means in terms of everyday living.

The intended convert arrived in the village during the 1940s from the Kigoma Region of Western Tanzania, a predominantly Muslim area adjoining Ujiji township. Upon arrival in Mto wa Mbu, he took a laborer's job on the *shamba* of one of the prosperous settlers. This resident was a Segeju from the coastal region, and a Muslim by birth, who was one of the earliest people to settle in the area.

After a few months, during which a number of discussions of religion took place, the newcomer requested further knowledge of Islam and expressed a desire to become a Muslim, with his employer as his religious sponsor. This was agreed upon, and after a few months the ceremony took place and the father-son relationship was established.

During this time the convert, who was then in his thirties, was in the process of clearing a field of his own, and was given the necessary tools by his sponsor. A short time later, he requested permission to marry; but since he was without funds, he had to rely completely on his sponsor's generosity. The man consented, and arranged a marriage with a daughter of one of his friends in the village, and paid the entire bride price, which amounted to a few hundred shillings. During the following years, the son continued to rely on his adopted father for aid in time of need. At one point the son injured his leg and the old man paid his fare to the city as well as the medical expenses involved until he was able to return to Mto wa Mbu. During this period his father also acted as sponsor to others and they became his brothers.

As the years passed and the young man established himself securely in the village, the relationship became less one sided. At the present time, the convert is in his fifties and is a well respected member of the community. He is also a TANU cell leader. He has a small *shamba*, plus a stall in the market where he sells tobacco and fruits. In addition, he buys fish and takes them to the city weekly where he resells them. He has purchased one of the new government built houses and has the honor of renting one of the rooms to the Muslim teacher.

On the other hand, the fortunes of the old man have turned. None of his natural sons have stayed with him and he is presently living with his last wife, the wife of his deceased son and his grandson. Since he is too old to cultivate and has no sons to farm for him, he has gradually sold off pieces of what was formerly a large holding. The remaining acreage is worked by casual laborers who receive a salary. The old man has difficulty walking, so his religious son visits him occasionally and gives him a few shillings or brings small items such as tea or sugar. He also takes fruits from the farm which he sells at his market stall, keeping some of the money for himself and returning some to the old man. The old man's wife and grandson visit the son's house to exchange greetings and local news almost daily.

The case serves to illustrate a number of factors which characterize this type of bond. As with all patron-client bonds, the client, in this case a potential convert, does not seek just anyone for his patron-sponsor, but tries to associate himself with someone in good standing in the community whom he will be able to rely upon in time of need. This represents a realistic appraisal by the newcomer of his own marginal social and economic position in the community. As in the case cited the migrant attempts to contract a relationship with one of the most prosperous and respected residents at the time and in doing so begins to establish himself in the community socially and protects himself from possible economic reverses until he is able to fend for himself.

In addition, the neophyte seeks to associate himself with a

resident who has a degree of religious prestige, one who is a Muslim by birth and from an area with a historical Islamic tradition. This was achieved when the convert chose as his sponsor a Muslim from the coastal area. In doing so, he was then able to associate with the Islamic reputation of this group. For the sponsor, the initial and important gains were ones of prestige since his reputation is enhanced by the number of converts he attracts to Islam and the number of new residents who defer to him. His position is also strengthened by the number of dependents he can call on in time of need for aid or favors.

Finally, this contract is similar to the biological one which ideally involves the same kind of reciprocity. At the outset the young man is dependent upon his father both socially and economically. As the years go by the quality of the relationship changes and the sponsor begins to depend on his son. Consequently, the relationship is balanced as the convert repays his sponsor for the advantages he has received in the past.

This contract, therefore, means gains for both parties if entered into by two individuals who fulfil the obligations. This new relationship with an established resident is the emigrant's visa into the social life of the community while it in turn further strengthens the position of the sponsor in the village. Both parties are assured a degree of economic security at the time when it is most vital, that is, when the convert first enters the village and when the sponsor reaches old age.

The discussion of this religious bond illustrates its similarity to other such relationships found in various parts of the world. Specifically, it could be compared with the formal *compadrazgo* tie important in many Catholic countries, especially in Latin America, or the more informal "patronage" networks characteristic of Mediterranean peasant societies. This aspect of social organization has received little attention in Africa, except where it has been an institutionalized feature of the traditional political system of stratified states. However, this type of relationship will become more apparent in African communities where kinship groups have become a relatively insignificant organizational feature.

CASE STUDIES

This final section presents a number of case studies. The examples presented below are representative of a larger number of in-depth interviews and illustrate typical life history patterns gathered from many other residents. They provide a concrete indication of the way in which marriage, kinship and religion can be seen as social processes affecting community organization. Further, they demonstrate at the personal level of experience how external developments, group affiliation and length of residence in Mto wa Mbu have affected the types of relationships built up by the migrant along the lines of religion, marriage and kinship. Two different types of residents emerged on the basis of the character of their primary social relationships: those who are community oriented and those who are externally oriented.

A. *Community Oriented Residents*

Mzee Hamisi is an elderly Muslim Segeju from Tanga Region on the coast of Tanzania. During his childhood he attended a German mission school for five years and learned a bit of German which he still remembers. After school and still a youth he worked on the German railroad which ran from Tanga to Mombo and later to Moshi. In doing so he saw a fair amount of the country.

While still in his teens he was chosen by the German colonial admini- stration as an *akida* (government representative and tax collector) and was sent to the then German territory of Ruanda-Burundi. While there the war broke out and he fought as a soldier on the German side. After the war he returned to Tanga, but he decided not to settle down and con- tinued his wanderings. He went to Tabora in Central Tanzania and then on to Ujiji and Kigoma in the western part of the country working at odd jobs. From there he returned to Tabora where he stayed for a few years before moving on to Engaruka, a small settlement in the Rift Valley about thirty miles north of Mto wa Mbu, where he had kinsmen. He stayed there for a few years farming as well as trading from a small shop. How- ever, the shop failed and he was not satisfied with his small farm. He de- cided to move to Mto wa Mbu where he heard the land was more plentiful and fertile. At this time when he was in his early thirties he decided to settle down in Mto wa Mbu and to clear a *shamba* which later grew to over fifty acres. He returned to Tanga where he married and then brought his wife to Mto wa Mbu. Later he called his mother's brother with whom he had lived in Engaruka to join him in Mto wa Mbu, and finally he called his brother from Tanga who then acted as the first Muslim teacher in the village.

During the following years while enlarging his holdings and improving his economic position, he became extremely influential in village affairs. In addition to marrying again to the daughter of another resident, he often employed new arrivals to the community to work on his land and aided many through hospitality, food and loan of tools to establish themselves in Mto wa Mbu. In return, through his influence many converted to Islam and chose him as their sponsor and patron thereby further enhancing his prestige among the inhabitants.

In 1969 all of his children had moved to other areas except for a divorced daughter and her children who were living with him and his wife. He had not returned to his original home in Tanga in over ten years, but his wife returns occasionally. Over the years he sold off parts of his land to new settlers and has retained only about twenty acres which are worked for him by casual laborers. He has few kinsmen left in the village, but he has many friends and expresses little interest in ever returning to Tanga.

Mzee Rashidi was born in 1910 in Kigoma Region of Western Tanzania and is a Ha. He spent his childhood and youth there farming and also herding his father's cattle. He was the third of six children and his father's second son. His father died when he was in his teens and his father's property was passed on to the eldest son.

In his early twenties he left his home to seek work in Arusha on a coffee estate. His main reason for leaving was to earn enough money to return home to purchase a few cows and to marry. However, he has not returned since the day he left.

He spent six years in Arusha working on European coffee estates and during this time he began living with a Sukuma girl who was staying there with her parents. When the girl's father died she went with her mother to Mto wa Mbu to live with her brother who was farming in the village. He followed the girl and while in Mto wa Mbu they married. They returned together to Arusha where he continued working, but after two years he decided to leave his work and return to Mto wa Mbu to farm among his wife's kinsmen. He stayed with them for a few months until he built himself a house and began to farm on his own. During his first year he was converted to Islam by one of his new acquaintances in the community.

After approximately ten years he divorced his wife who then returned to Arusha. He kept the children with him and married again. Again, this marriage lasted for ten years before they separated. At this time in his late fifties he married again to a young Gorowa girl who was living in Mto wa Mbu with her mother's sister.

At the present time he is living with his young wife in one of the new houses built by the government which was purchased by his eldest son. He still has his farm, but spends most of his time in the market selling tobacco and some produce. His two surviving sons have settled in Arusha and Dar es Salaam and they visit him occasionally. Frequently he buys a load of fish from the fisherman in the village and takes them to Arusha for resale. During these trips he stays with his son, daughter-in-law and grandchildren for a few days before returning.

In Mto wa Mbu he is a respected member of the Muslim community and a party leader. He considers Mto wa Mbu his home because of his long absence from his place of birth and the lack of contact with his kinsmen. He says that he would like to return home someday for a visit but that he has no intentions of staying there.

Mzee Salim was born in Sukumaland about 1905. Towards the end of the war he was a porter in the German army. After the war he returned to his home, but stayed for only a few months before going to Nairobi where he found work as a road laborer. He remained in Kenya for four years and then left for Tanga in Tanzania where he had relatives. After a stay of one year he sought work as a laborer on the new railroad link between Moshi and Arusha. The line reached Arusha in three years where it terminated and he decided to stay. While there he heard from other Sukuma that there were members of his ethnic group living in Mto wa Mbu. Hearing that good land was available he decided to try his luck rather than return to Sukuma country.

He arrived in the village some time in the early 1930s still a young man and took up residence in the house of a fellow tribesman. While living there he helped out on the farm and in his spare time used his friend's tools to clear a farm of his own. After a year he built a house on his land and began to cultivate for himself. When he arrived he was a Pagan, but after a few years he was converted to Islam by an Nguu from the coast. He then married a Muslim Gogo who was living in the village with her parents. After she bore three children he divorced her and remarried. One of his children is married and moved to Arusha and another son has married and now lives in Sukumaland.

He feels that he might like to return to his home someday, but at present is satisfied with his life in Mto wa Mbu. He said if his older brother were to die he would return home to inherit cattle, but otherwise he would remain in Mto wa Mbu.

Although a Nyamwezi Juma was born in Kondoa where his father had moved to farm. While in Kondoa and cultivating part of his father's land he married. In 1953 when he was about twenty-five he moved to Mto wa Mbu with his father, his own wife and his unmarried younger brother and sister. During this time he cleared his own *shamba* and set up a household on his own.

In 1964 he divorced his first wife and remarried a young girl who was living in Mto wa Mbu with her parents. He had no children by his first wife, but had three by his second. Since arriving both his brother and sister have married in the community and continue to live there.

Having studied with a *mwalimu* (teacher) for a number of years while in Kondoa, he earned the title of *mwalimu* for himself. He takes a great interest in religious affairs and is a respected member of the Muslim community. Since most of his important kinsmen live with him, he takes little interest in the others outside of the community.

Mzee Mohammed was born in Singida around 1910. He was the second son of his father and was born a Muslim. When he was eighteen years old he left home and went to live with his elder brother who was working on a plantation outside of Moshi. He stayed with him for a few months but failing to find work he left to look for work near Arusha. He then found employment as a gardener on a European farm and stayed for five years.

He left there to look for work in Oldeani where there was a European settlement; however, since he was on foot he decided to stop and rest in Mto wa Mbu. He was offered a job herding goats in Mto wa Mbu and he took it intending to stay for a short time. He then took a job as the servant of an Indian who opened the first *duka* (shop) in the village. After 1944 he married an Iramba girl who was in Mto wa Mbu with her parents and left his job to begin farming. He lived with her for ten years and had three children. Then he divorced his wife and married again to a Rangi girl who was living in Mto wa Mbu with her parents after leaving her first husband. Since then he has had five more children who are still young and live with him. His son of the first marriage is living and farming in the village while his two daughters have married; one has remained in Mto wa Mbu and the other has moved with her husband.

He has only returned to Singida where his younger sister is living with her husband on their father's farm for short visits. He has no intention of returning to Singida because he says he is a *mgeni* (stranger) there while in Mto wa Mbu he is a *mwenyeji* (resident).

Mzee Mkulima was born in Sukumaland in 1908 as the second son of his father's first wife. He remained home until he married his first wife and started cultivating his own part of his father's *shamba*. After his first child was born he left home to seek work on the coast as a farm laborer. He stayed for one year and then went on to Arusha where one of his kinsmen was farming. While living in Arusha he heard of Mto wa Mbu from residents who had come to Arusha to sell fish from Lake Manyara and decided to move again. When he arrived, he lived for a few months with some of his clansmen before building his own house.

After two years he married a Sukuma girl who had recently arrived with her parents. They remained together for ten years before separating and the children stayed with him. He then married again to an Mbugwe girl and after two years in 1951 he became a Catholic. His two children of this marriage are still young and living with him, but his son of his second wife married in Mto wa Mbu and then moved to Tanga. His daughter married in Mto wa Mbu and had two children before her husband divorced her and converted from Catholicism to Islam. He now lives with his third wife and their young children and his divorced daughter and her children.

Since leaving Sukuma country over forty years ago he has returned only once and expresses no interest in returning again. Besides members of his own clan and his children, he has no other kinsmen in Mto wa Mbu.

Although no two of the above examples are exactly alike, a number of general, but important, similarities are apparent. First, the majority are long-term residents whose initial decision to leave home was somehow prompted by the changes brought on by the introduction of the colonial regime either in the form of direct participation in the European social system or by wage labor in order to meet the demands of taxation. Second, the common denominator of Islam appears in almost all of the cases. If not born a Muslim, at some time during their wanderings Islam was accepted. For those who entered the community as traditionalists conversion to Islam followed shortly with the single Catholic the only exception to the rule. Third, the contracting of a marriage within Mto wa Mbu to the daughter of an established resident is also a prevalent feature.

These last two factors of conversion and marriage are indications of decisions on the part of these then new settlers to establish a series of important relationships within the confines of the village and thereby participate more fully in the social life of the community. Over time these relationships began to assume greater importance than the traditional ones which maintained the migrant's ties to his former home. In effect his social orientation was directed inward and greater participation in religious, political and social affairs of the community followed. This can be compared to the following case histories.

B. *Externally Oriented Residents*

Daudi was born a Christian in 1924 in the Machame Area of Chagga District. He was the fifth of six male children and the third son of his father's second wife. When he was still a child his father died and he was raised by his mother who remained a widow. In 1940 when he was twenty-six years old he married at home to a Chagga girl and began cultivating bananas and coffee on a half-acre plot which was his inheritance from his father. Since his father only owned three acres, each of the sons received one half of an acre.

In 1944 he joined the King's African Rifles and was stationed in Nairobi until 1946. He returned home and remained there until 1948 when he decided that he would employ his skill learned in the military and take a job as a mason working on various odd jobs in Northern Tanzania. He continued this for twelve years and in 1960 while passing through the village on his way home he inquired of some Chagga living in Mto wa Mbu about the prospects of getting a *shamba*.

Having heard good reports he returned in 1961 and bought an uncleared piece of land for 130 shillings ($18.). He cleared the land and built a house and later brought his wife and four youngest children to live with him. He left his oldest son and daughter with his brother at home in Machame to look after his small plot of coffee since it brings in a cash income.

Although he is satisfied with his new and larger farm in Mto wa Mbu, he plans to return to Machame to live among his kinsmen. When all of his children have reached adulthood and are no longer economically dependent on him he says he will give his *shamba* in Mto wa Mbu to whichever of his sons wants it or divide it among them and return to his half acre at home where he plans to spend his remaining days.

Charles was born of Protestant parents in 1938 in the Meru Area just west of Arusha as the fourth son of his father's third wife. When he was eleven he started school and completed four years. He then started working for a mason as an apprentice in Meru for two years. Having learned the trade he left for the District Headquarters in Monduli, but could not find work. He finally found employment in a small retail shop for one and a half years before returning home for a few months. He later returned home again to be initiated with his age set and remained for six months.

At the end of this period he married a Meru girl and lived there with her for one year. After the birth of a child he departed for Moshi to seek employment. He found work as a laborer on a farm outside of Moshi for one year before returning home again for a brief period. He left again for Monduli where he worked as a mason for another two years. While in Monduli he took another wife who was a Gorowa and had parents living in Mto wa Mbu. In 1963 he arrived in Mto wa Mbu to visit his wife's parents and stayed with a friend for a few days before returning to Monduli. After one month he returned with his second wife and bought a four acre *shamba* for 400 shillings ($56.).

He spends his day farming and gets occasional jobs as a mason. He has had three children by his second wife while in Mto wa Mbu. He divorced his first wife and his son by that marriage lives with his grandmother in Meru.

He still retains a small farm in Meru which he inherited at the death of his father. The three acres which were his share are being tended to by a younger brother in his absence. Each year he returns home to inspect the coffee crop since he intends to return to stay one day. During these stays he visits with his close family including his first wife. He has no kinsmen in Mto wa Mbu.

Isa is a forty year old Rangi born in Kondoa District in Central Tanzania. He has been a Muslim since birth as are the great majority of Rangi in Mto wa Mbu. While in Kondoa as a young man he married and was farming; however, he also took a job as a laborer for the government's road maintenance division. His work took him away from his home to other parts of the country and finally to where he was stationed in 1956, Mto wa Mbu. While in the village he decided to give up his job and farm. He felt that cultivating in the area could supply him with enough food and cash to make his job unnecessary. Consequently, he called his wife and one child to Mto wa Mbu and left his eldest son with his father in Kondoa to take care of his cattle. At the same time he turned over his *shamba* at home to his brother.

After two years he returned home to marry a second wife and returned with her to Mto wa Mbu. During his first few months in the village he met many he had known previously while working and he also met a fellow clansman. However, he did not know that they were living in the community when he decided to stay. Although he had given up his fields at home, he still retains a great interest in his cattle to the extent of making four or five trips per year to inspect them while visiting with his father and son.

In 1969 he had been living in the village for twelve years and considered it his new home. He has many ties in the village through Islam including his few kinsmen and the numerous Rangi who have settled in Mto wa Mbu. Nevertheless, his frequent trips to Kondoa to check on his cattle and visit with his close family also indicates strong interests in the place of his birth. When talking about Kondoa he always refers to it as *kwetu* (our home).

He has not made up his mind as to whether or not he will ever return to Kondoa to live which means he still does not consider Mto wa Mbu a permanent home. He stated that if farming was as easy in Kondoa as it is in Mto wa Mbu, he would return immediately because Kondoa District is "home." However, the fact that his family is secure in Mto wa Mbu is more important to him than returning.

Stephen is a Pare born in the Pare hills in 1932 where he farmed until 1962 when he moved to Mto wa Mbu. He was prompted to make the move because his father who did mission work was stationed in a small village twenty miles away and in 1961 he had bought a small *shamba* in Mto wa Mbu. In 1962 his father asked him to move to the village to help in cultivating. He arrived with his wife and children and immediately bought a three acre *shamba* for himself and was given another one and a half acres adjoining it for clearing.

A short time later he was joined by his two brothers and their families. They were followed in turn by his father's brother and his sons and then his mother's brother. All have their own farms and a number of his younger kinsmen returned to the Pare hills to marry and returned with their wives. However, two daughters of his father's brother have returned home to marry and have remained there with their husbands.

He and all of his kinsmen are members of the small Seventh Day Adventist Church and form a close-knit group. He intends to remain in Mto wa Mbu, but he hopes his children will return home to marry Pare girls rather than marry in the community. He feels that he has a much better life here since his *shamba* in the Pare hills was small, difficult to farm and subjected to soil erosion.

While in Mto wa Mbu he opened a small tailor's shop, but it has failed. In 1969 he left his wife and children and opened another shop in a town fifty miles away. He felt that there were greater opportunities there, but he intends to leave his family on his *shamba* in Mto wa Mbu and return as often as possible for visits.

Rajabu was born in Kondoa District a Muslim in 1928. He was the last of six children and the third son. When he was eighteen years old he married a Rangi girl and began cultivating his own eight acres from his

father's *shamba*. He remained at home for ten years and married another
Rangi girl. By this time he had a total of four children.

At the age of twenty-eight he left home to look for work. He first went
to Dodoma where his mother's brother was living, but he could not find
employment. He stayed for a while and then went on to Dar es Salaam
for a short period before journeying to Pemba Island where he found
work as a laborer on a plantation. He remained there for one and a half
years before returning to Kondoa. He stayed for only a short time and
then in 1961 leaving his wives and children behind he moved on to Mto
wa Mbu where another of his mother's brothers was living.

He stayed with him until he received his own piece of land which he
cleared and then started to cultivate. After two years when his field was
beginning to produce, he married a third time to a Makonde girl who was
born in Mto wa Mbu. He has left his first two wives at home, but he visits
them regularly.

The individuals portrayed in these case histories have failed
for the most part to be drawn into social relationships within the
community. This is partially due to their reasons for leaving home.
In the first studies the migrants left their original homes in some
way as a response to the demands of the colonial system. The
second group, on the other hand, in most instances was able to
adjust to this system without abandoning traditional pursuits.
It was not until the internal pressures of land shortage and soil
erosion as a result of overpopulation initiated some adjustments
that these people began to migrate from their traditional areas or
failed to return to it after a period away as wage earners. In effect,
these people were grudgingly forced from their land while the
community oriented residents of Mto wa Mbu chose to abandon
their traditional homes.

The external orientation of the second group of settlers is
further indicated by the economic interest they have retained in
their former homes. The small coffee plots or few head of cattle
if they must be abandoned by the owner are left in the care of
some close member of the family, such as a wife, child or brother.
Therefore, the economic tie to the place of origin is strengthened
by its coexistence with a kinship link. These factors necessitate
periodic visits home to insure the state of both kin and property.
A crucial point illustrated in a number of the cases is that the
active maintenance of these social and economic investments allows

the migrant to retain the option of returning home permanently at a later date.

The failure of these individuals to contract marriages within Mto wa Mbu is a further indication of their lack of commitment to the community. There is a definite inclination to choose a wife from home instead of Mto wa Mbu which adds to existing ties outside of the village rather than creates new ones within it.

A careful reading of these cases for both types of residents shows that these two categories are not mutually exclusive. Some individuals' case histories show a mixed-type of orientation. Rajabu's history is a perfect illustration. Although he has retained control over his fields in Kondoa and has left his first two wives and children there, he has taken a co-resident as a third wife from a different ethnic group. Nevertheless, there are some differences to be recognized among the inhabitants concerning the tendency to maximize or minimize possible relationships within the community.

The studies indicate that considered as groups there is a significant age differential between the community oriented and externally oriented residents. The exact figures when available indicate that for the first category the ages range from 45 to 65 years while for the other from 32 to 46 years.

This could lead to two different conclusions. It could be assumed that the younger inhabitants having lived in the community for a shorter period of time have not yet had the time to develop the kind of network of relationships exemplified by the older group. This would mean that the type of orientation is merely a function of the passage of time. To an extent time is a crucial dimension for it is not possible to develop a social network centered in the community within a short period. Ties based on participation in a religious congregation, the contraction of a marriage to a resident and even those of kinship take time to cultivate.

On the other hand, and this is closely related to the first factor, those individuals who had not developed these internal relationships had left Mto wa Mbu and returned home before reaching their later years. This would mean that a selective factor is in operation so that the residents of long standing are those who made an early decision to remain in Mto wa Mbu. Whether this was made before or after these ties were established would be difficult to determine. Possibly the decision to remain and con-sider Mto wa Mbu a permanent home was the result of ties that bound. At the same time discussions with residents and the figures on the ethnic composition of the village suggest that many former inhabitants have returned to their original home. These individuals could have been described at the time they were in Mto wa Mbu as externally oriented.

8

TRIBALISM AND THE RURAL CENTER

Studies of culturally heterogeneous urban centers in Africa have clearly demonstrated that ethnic groups have emerged as a significant feature of urban social organization. The relevant literature indicates that migrants to the city consider common cultural identity and traditional relationships as important bases for interaction and the framework for the creation of formal associations. Epstein (1958) and Watson (1958), among others, have shown that during the colonial period urban "tribalism" was not a vestige of the past, but instead a viable social mechanism for dealing with the problems posed by migration and wage labor. Recent reports indicate that the political withdrawal of the Europeans has not had the effect of de-emphasizing the importance of shared ethnicity. Parkin (1969) writes that, just prior to independence, Luo and Luyha Kenyans in Kampala exhibited a heightened sense of ethnic solidarity in response to anticipated threats to their alien status in Uganda. Cohen (1969) also points out that, in independent Nigeria, Hausa minorities have continued to retain their cultural identity in Yoruba dominated communities and have utilized common ethnicity in the attempt to monopolize trade between the countryside and town.

This process of employing traditional cultural symbols for the purpose of emphasizing ethnic distinctiveness, Cohen (1969) defines as "retribalization."

The descriptions of other commentators on the urban scene

in Africa provide supportive evidence for Cohen's conclusions. Yet, this process of "retribalization" is not a characteristic social process in Mto wa Mbu. In addition, Vincent's (1971) study of local-level politics in the poly-ethnic village of Gondo in Uganda also pointed up the unimportance of ethnicity in the rural setting. Generalizing from the descriptions of these two rural cases, it would seem that contemporary African ethnic politics is fostered by the social forces at work in urban centers. The existence of a large population of the same ethnic background provides a necessary precondition for the process of "retribalization," while the competition over scarce economic and political rewards provides the stimulus. On the other hand, Mto wa Mbu, with its multiple ethnic isolates, each with limited numerical strength, does not provide an opportune setting for "retribalization" nor are the needs of small-scale cultivation facilitated by it. The special case of the Chagga in Mto wa Mbu who can be described as having "retribalized" does not contradict this argument for their primary concern is control over small-scale trade in the community. In this way their behavior resembles that of other ethnic groups in urban areas.

On this basis it may be argued that cities in Africa provide a conservative atmosphere since in some instances they tend to restrict the individual's political commitment to an ethnic group rather than the state. If there is a "melting pot" in terms of proding a national consciousness it may be located in rural African centers where ethnicity is a less significant factor of community social organization. Therefore, certain aspects of what is generally considered to be modernization are being expressed more vigorously in the countryside than in the city. In any event, the idea that rural areas are inherently conservative while urban centers are characteristically progressive can not be accepted uncritically. Since many of the independent nations of Africa, Tanzania included, are concentrating their resources on rural as opposed to urban development, there may be a number of unintended practical political consequences to be gained by this policy.

RURAL DEVELOPMENT

From a sociological orientation a lack of ethnic consciousness and the absence of such groups in a community is neither a positive nor negative state of affairs. It is simply a problem for analysis. However, from the standpoint of a government which is attempting to create a nation where none existed before it is another matter. For African governments, "tribalism," whether considered to be an indigenous feature or a product of the colonial experience, is an anathema. President Nyerere of Tanzania speaking just after his country received its independence said: "We find that our country must learn to think as a nation, and we are faced with the question of organization and of getting the 120 tribes to think of themselves as one people" (quoted in Burke 1965).

In order to achieve this goal the Tanzanian administration has embarked on an ambitious development program aimed primarily at improving the lot of the people living in the countryside. It was decided that this could be done most efficiently if a greater segment of the rural population were located in more compact settlements than traditionally found in the countryside where a scattered residential pattern was the general rule. This policy of planned charge has in some instances involved the creation of new communities through government sponsorship and direct aid. In others, the expansion of existing villages has been encouraged in a variety of ways. However, of late the entire program, and especially the area of government initiated projects, has become the object of critical evaluation.

Seen from this perspective the village of Mto wa Mbu takes on a new relevance. How is it that a settlement formed and developed without any outside aid, where the residents come from every conceivable part of the country but think of themselves not as *watu wa Kabiha* (tribesmen) but as *wananchi* (citizens), emerges as a model village for the Tanzania of the future? Even the new goals of the government such as cooperative labor and ownership of land rather than individualized holdings has become a reality in Mto wa Mbu in recent years. On the other hand, government sponsored projects which were designed to become model communities have been in the main failures. Some answers to this

puzzle are suggested from a comparison of Mto wa Mbu to government project settlements.

There are various types of government programs in existence:
some are based on collective labor while others on private agricultural holdings; some involve the settling of individuals in a new
district or area while a number involve villagization in the traditional area of the people involved (Apthorpe 1968). They are all
similar, however, to the extent that they have involved intensive
planning and direct aid in the form of personnel and capital. It
was hoped that after a period of time the outside experts would
be replaced by residents while the government's initial capital investment would be repaid over a period of years from the profits
derived from the sale of the community's livestock or agricultural
produce.

Another characteristic of these development schemes, although
not to the same degree, is that the members of the new community are usually from the same ethnic group or at least overwhelmingly so even if the resettlement involves the exploitation
of a virgin area. For example, the Upper Kitete wheat scheme of
Mbulu District in Northern Tanzania is typical, since 97 of the
100 families are Iraqw, who form the major part of the District's
population.

These settlement schemes, unfortunately, also have one further
characteristic in common—their failure to achieve stated goals.
A few short years after its conception, the entire program was
declared somewhat less than even a moderate success by the
Tanzanian government, and by 1965 it had been considerably deemphasized as an aspect of rural development policy (Morris
1968). The decision to under-cut this program was based on a
number of factors, not the least being economic considerations.
In Tanzania the typical scheme involved an initial capital investment by the government of approximately 150,000 pounds
($420,000.) to benefit 250 families, with the aim of recovering
125,000 pounds ($350,000) over a twenty-five year period. By
1968, it was realized that such an assumption was highly optimistic (Moris 1968). The term optimistic is probably an understate-
ment, since at one such scheme I was informed by the manager
that not only would they not be in a position to return a portion of
the initial capital investment of 100,000 pounds, but they could not

completely repay that year's government advance for operating expenses. If this is a typical example, then the cost to the government for these projects is much more than the original investment of 450,000 pounds and is a continual drain on the budget. In addition to being an economic failure, it was also discovered that these schemes produced among the members an opposite effect than that which was intended since the participants came to rely on the government rather than become self-reliant. In the attempt to generate a degree of political consciousness the results were also disappointing. Despite the frequent presence of government officials and even visits from numerous touring foreign heads of state the inhabitants took little interest in political matters.

As a contrast, in Mto wa Mbu almost one thousand families have raised their standard of living at no expense to the government by settling in and developing the community largely on their own initiative. Why this is the case while government aided settlements have been less fruitful involves numerous considerations beyond the scope of this study. These government schemes have been the object of intensive investigation by social scientists (Apthorpe 1968) and it has become apparent that considerations concerned with over capitalization, lack of planning, poor management and a host of other elements are involved. Since this study has been concerned only with Mto wa Mbu from a purely sociological perspective, any suggestions must necessarily stem from this basis.

Therefore, I would prefer to return again to the fact that Mto wa Mbu is intensively heterogeneous while the settlement scheme communities usually are not. The aim of the government program was not only economic for it was an integral part of the overall attempt to produce a modern state, and, therefore, these schemes had political and social goals as well. It was hoped that these projects would generate a sense of community among their residents and from this base the more general goal of a sense of identity with the state (Nyerere 1967). It seems realistic to propose that the ethnic exclusivity of these settlement scheme communities has hampered the development of this sense of identity and at the same time diminished the effectiveness of self-help projects within them. The failure to stimulate a new sense of communal, and thence national, identity seems to be a reflection of their ethnic composition. I would hazard the assumption that in these settlement villages the typical social network of the residents is very similar to that described for the externally oriented network of a portion of the inhabitants of Mto wa Mbu. In effect, the social field of the residents is contained within the framework of traditional relationships and from there diverted away from the settlement into the surrounding countryside. For example, Thomas (n.d.) suggests that in Upper Kitete the families may have been "resettled but not uprooted." As a result, the sense of primary identity with their ethnic group and traditional relationships remains paramount to that of the community and state.

On the other hand, in Mto wa Mbu the residents are quick to point out their differences as a community from the surrounding population and they take a certain amount of pride in their political sophistication and status as *wananchi*. Further, there is little or no trouble in achieving the necessary cooperation required for village self-help development projects. This is at least partially due to the fact that traditional goals and the means of achieving them have gone the way of traditional relationships, neither of which are viable in Mto wa Mbu. Along with the necessity of creating new types of ties has been the acceptance of a new sense of identity and different values which also conform to those of the state. It is not surprising, therefore, that the residents call themselves *Waswahili*, a term which implies people without a tribe. In the past, this had negative connotations, but since independence the opposite is true. In a sense, then, the people of Mto wa Mbu have been Tanzanians before there was a Tanzania. The hope of achieving the same conditions in ethnically homogeneous settlements would be a much more difficult and complex process.

The relevance of Mto wa Mbu to the contemporary problems of rural development lies primarily in its poly-ethnic character. If, as Nyerere says, Tanzania must mold a nation from over 120 different ethnic groups, then, wherever possible, development projects, capital and energies should be aimed at producing this type of community at the local level.

REFERENCES

Abrahams, R.G.
   1961   "Kahama Township, Western Province, Tanganyika,"
          in *Social Change in Modern Africa* (ed. Aidan Southall).
          London: Oxford University Press.
Apthorpe, Raymond
   1968   "Planned Social Change and Land Settlement." *Nkanga*
          3:5-13.
Arens, W.
   1973   "Tribalism and the Poly-Ethnic Rural Community."
          Man (N.S.). 8:441-450.
   1975a "The Waswahili: The Social History of an Ethnic
          Group." *Africa* 45:426-438.
   1975b "Islam and Christianity in sub-Saharan Africa: Ethnog-
          raphic Reality or Ideology." *Cahiers d'Études Africaines*
          15:443-456.
   1976   "Changing Patterns of Ethnic Identity and Prestige in
          Contemporary East Africa," in *A Century of Change in
          Eastern Africa* (ed. W. Arens). The Hague: Mouton.
Arens, W. and Arens, Diana Antos
   1978   "Kinship and Marriage in a Polyethnic Community."
          Africa 48:149-160.
Banton, Michael
   1957   *West African City.* London: Oxford University Press.
Bates, M.L.
   1965   "Tanganyika: Changes in African Life, 1918-1945," in
          History of East Africa (eds. Vincent Harlow and E.M.
          Chilver). Vol. II. Oxford: The Clarendon Press.

Bohannan, Paul
  1964   *Africa and Africans.* Garden City: The Natural History Press.
Brandel, M.
  1959   "Urban *Lobolo* Attitudes." *African Studies* 17:34-50.
Brewin, D.R.
  1964   "Kilimanjaro Agriculture." *Tanzania Notes and Records* 64:115-117.
Brokensha, David W.
  1966   *Social Change at Larteh, Ghana.* Oxford: The Clarendon Press.
Burke, Fred G.
  1965   *Tanganyika Preplanning.* Syracuse: Syracuse University Press.
Cohen, Abner
  1969   *Custom and Politics in Urban Africa.* London: Routledge and Kegan Paul.
Cohen, Ronald and Middleton, John (eds.)
  1970   *From Tribe to Nation in Africa.* Scranton: Chandler Publishing Company.
Coupland, Sir Reginald
  1968   *The Exploitation of East Africa 1856-1890.* London: Faber and Faber Limited.
Epstein, A.L.
  1958   *Politics in an Urban African Community.* Manchester: Manchester University Press.
  1967   "Urbanization and Social Change in Africa." *Current Anthropology* 8:275-295.
Firth, Raymond
  1959   *Social Change in Tikopia.* London: George Allen and Unwin.
  1964   *Essays on Social Organization and Values.* London: The Athlone Press.
Fraenkel, Merran
  1964   *Tribe and Class in Monrovia.* London: Oxford University Press for I.A.I.
Gray, Robert F.
  1963   *The Sonjo of Tanganyika.* London: Oxford University Press for I.A.I.

Guillotte, Joseph
1970 *Personal Communication.* (In author's possession).
Gulliver, P.H.
1959 "A Tribal Map of Tanganyika." *Tanganyika Notes and Records* 52:61-74.
1969a "The Conservative Commitment in Northern Tanzania: The Arusha and Masai," in *Tradition and Transition in East Africa* (ed. P.H. Gulliver). London: Routledge and Kegan Paul.
1969b "Introduction," in *Tradition and Transition in East Africa* (ed. P.H. Gulliver). London: Routledge and Kegan Paul.
Gutkind, Peter C.W.
1965 "African Urbanism, Mobility and the Social Network," in *Kinship and Geographical Mobility* (ed. Ralph Piddington). Leiden: E.J. Brill.
Harries, Lyndon
1964 "The Arabs and Swahili Culture." *Africa* 34:224-229.
Harris, J.H.
1951 "Lake Manyara." *Tanganyika Notes and Records* 30:6-14.
Hellman, E.
1948 *Rooiyard.* (*Rhodes-Livingston Papers,* No. 13). Capetown: Oxford University Press.
Hino, S.
1968 "The Costume Culture of the Swahili People." *Kyoto University African Studies* 2:109-145.
Horton, Robin
1971 "African Conversion." *Africa* 12:85-108.
International Bank for Reconstruction and Development.
1961 *The Economic Development of Tanganyika.* Baltimore: The Johns Hopkins Press.
Ishige, Naomichi
1969 "On Swahilization." *Kyoto University African Studies* 3:94-109.
Johnson, P.H.
1946 "Some Notes on Land Tenure in Kilimanjaro and the *Vihamba* of the Wachagga." *Tanganyika Notes and Records* 21:1-20.

Kimambo, Isaria N.
1969 *A Political History of the Pare of Tanzania 1500-1900.*
Nairobi: East African Publishing House.

Lewis, I.M.
1966 "Introduction," in *Islam in Tropical Africa* (ed. I.M.
Lewis). London: Oxford University Press for I.A.I.

Lienhardt, Peter
1968 *The Medicine Man.* Oxford: The Clarendon Press.

Little, Kenneth
1967 "Voluntary Associations in Urban Life," in *Social
Organization* (ed. Maurice Freedman). Chicago: Aldine
Publishing Company.

Long, Norman
1968 *Social Change and the Individual.* Manchester: Manchester University Press.

Low, D.A.
1963 "The Northern Interior, 1840-1884," in *History of
East Africa.* (eds. Roland Oliver and G. Matthews).
Vol. I. Oxford: The Clarendon Press.

Marris, Peter
1961 *Family and Social Change in an African City.* London:
Routledge and Kegan Paul.

Masai District Book, Northern Province, Tanganyika Territory.
(Located in Masai-Monduli Headquarters. Monduli,
Tanzania).

Masai District Records. Northern Province, Tanganyika Territory.
(Located in Masai-Monduli Headquarters. Monduli,
Tanzania).

Mayer, Philip
1963 *Townsmen or Tribesmen.* Cape Town: Oxford University Press.

Mitchell, J.C.
1956 "The Kalela Dance." *Rhodes-Livingston Papers,* no. 27.
Published on Behalf of Rhodes-Livingston Institute by
Manchester University Press.
1957 "Aspects of African Marriage in the Copper Belt."
Rhodes-Livingston Journal 22:1-30.
1966 "Theoretical Orientations in African Urban Studies," in
The Social Anthropology of Complex Societies. (ed.

Michael Banton). A.S.A. Monographs, No. 4. London: Tavistock Publications.

1970 "Tribe and Social Change in South Central Africa: A Situational Approach," in *The Passing of Tribal Man in Africa* (ed. Peter Gutkind). Leiden: E.J. Brill.

Moris, J.
1968 "The Evaluation of Settlement Schemes Performance: A Sociological Appraisal." *Nkanga* 3:79-102.

Murdock, George P.
1959 *Africa: Its Peoples and Their Culture History.* New York: McGraw-Hill Publishing Co.

Nyerere, Julius
1967 *Freedom and Unity.* London: Oxford University Press.
1968 *Ujamaa:Essays on Socialism.* Dar es Salaam: Oxford University Press.

Omar, Saada Salim bin
1940 "The Swahili Life," *Tanganyika Notes and Records* 9:20-26.

Parkin, David
1968 "Medicines and Men of Influence." *Man* (N.S.) 3:424-439.
1969 *Neighbors and Nationals in an African City Ward.* London: Routledge and Kegan Paul.

Pike, A.G.
1964 "Kilimanjaro and the Furrow System." *Tanzania Notes and Records* 64:95-96.

Plotnicov, Leonard
1967 *Strangers to the City.* Pittsburgh: University of Pittsburgh Press.

Pons, Valdo
1969 *Stanleyville.* London: Oxford University Press.

Prins, A.H.J.
1967 *The Swahili-Speaking Peoples of Zanzibar and the East African Coast.* London: International African Institute.

Reusch, R.
1953 "How the Swahili People and Language Came into Existence." *Tanganyika Notes and Records* 34:20-27.

Roberts, Andrew
1968 "The Nyamwezi," in *Tanzania Before 1900.* (ed.

Andrew Roberts).Nairobi: East African Publishing House.

Sassoon, H.

1967 "New Views on Engaruka, Northern Tanzania." *Journal of African History* 8:201-217.

Shorthose, W.T. Captain

1923 *Sport and Adventure in Africa.* London: Seeley, Service and Co. Ltd.

Sofer, C. and Sofer, R.

1955 *Jinga Transformed.* Kampala: East African Institute of Social Research.

Southall, Aidan

1961a "Introductory Summary," in *Social Change in Modern Africa.* (ed. Aidan Southall). London: Oxford University Press for I.A.I.

1961b "Population Movements in East Africa," in *Essays on African Population.* (eds. K.M. Barbour and R.M. Prothero) London: Routledge and Kegan Paul.

Southall, Aidan and Gutkind, Peter C.W.

1957 *Townsmen in the Making.* Kampala: East African Institute of Social Research.

Steel, R.W.

1961 "The Towns of Tropical Africa," in *Essays on African Population.* (eds. K.M. Barbour and R.M. Prothero). London: Routledge and Kegan Paul.

Tanner, R.E.S.

1964 "Cousin Marriage in the Afro-Arab Community of Mombasa, Kenya." *Africa* 34:127-138.

Thomas, Garry

"Upper Kitete: A Communal Wheat Scheme." Unpublished Ms. (In author's possession).

Trimingham, J. Spencer

1962 *Islam in East Africa.* London: Edinburgh House Press.

1964 *Islam in East Africa.* Oxford: Clarendon Press.

1968 *The Influence of Islam on Africa.* London: Longmans, Green and Co. Ltd.

Van Velsen, J.

1961 "Labour Migration as a Positive Factor in the Continuity of Tonga Tribal Society," in *Social Change in Modern Africa.* (ed. Aidan Southall). London: Oxford

University Press for I.A.I.

Vincent, Joan
  1971   *African Elite: The Big Men of a Small Town.* New York:
          Columbia University Press.

von Clemm, Michael
  1964   "Agricultural Productivity and Sentiment on Kili-
          manjaro." *Economic Botany* 18:99-121.

Watermeyer, A.M. and Elliot, H.F.I.
  1943   "Lake Manyara." *Tanganyika Notes and Records* 15:
          58-71.

Watson, William
  1958   *Tribal Cohesion in a Money Economy.* Manchester:
          Manchester University Press.
  1967   "Tribalism and Labor Migration," Paper read at the
          Meetings of African Studies Association, New York.
          (In author's possession).

Wazaki, Yoiti
  1966   "Chama: An African Native Concept of Group Inte-
          gration—A Case of a Little Village 'Mongola,' Tanzania."
          Kyoto University African Studies 1:231-255.

Weber, Max
  1958   "The Protestant Sects and the Spirit of Capitalism," in
          From Max Weber (eds. Hans Gerth and C.W. Mills). New
          York: Oxford University Press.

Willis, R.G.
  1968   "Kamcape: An Anti-Sorcery Movement in South-West
          Tanzania." *Africa* 28:1-15.

Wilson, Godfrey
  1942   *An Essay on the Economics of Detribalization.* (Rhodes-
          Livingstone Papers No. 6). Capetown: Oxford Univer-
          sity Press.

Wilson, Gordon
  1961   "Mombasa—A Modern Colonial Municipality," in *Social
          Change in Modern Africa.* (ed. Aidan Southall). London:
          Oxford University Press for I.A.I.

Wijeyewardene, G.E.T.
  1958   *A Preliminary Report on Tribal Differentiation and
          Social Groupings on the Southern Kenyan Coast.*
          Paper read at the Meetings of the East African Institute

of Social Research. Makerere College: Kampala. (In author's possession).

1959a *Kinship and Ritual in the Swahili Community.* Paper read at the Meetings of the East African Institute of Social Research. Pangani: Tanzania. (In author's possession).

1959b *Manburi: Status and Social Relations in a Multi-Racial Community.* Paper read at the Meetings of the East African Institute of Social Research, Makerere College: Kampala. (In author's possession).

1959c *Administration and Politics in Two Swahili Communities.* Paper read at the Meetings of the East African Institute of Social Research. Makerere College: Kampala. (In author's possession).

Winter, E.H.
1955 *Bwamba Economy.* Kampala: East African Institute of Social Research.

Winter, E.H. and Molyneaux, Lambert
1963 "Population Patterns and Problems Among the Iraqw." *Ethnology* 11:490-505.

Wittfogel, Karl A.
1957 *Oriental Despotism.* New Haven: Yale University Press.

DT
449
M7
A73
1979

Arens, W., 1940-
   On the frontier of change Mto Wa
Mbu, Tanzania / William Arens. -- Ann
Arbor : University of Michigan Press :
produced and distributed by University
Microfilms International, c1979.
   xii, 150 p. : ill., maps ; 23 cm. --
(Monograph publishing : Imprint
series) ([LCAnthropology series)

   A revision of the author's thesis,
University of Virginia, 1970.
   Bibliography: p. [143]-150.
   ISBN 0-472-02714-X : $10.00

(Cont'd on next card)

MUNION ME   811023   811022 CStoC
R000217   EB /UPG   A*   81-B396
                               79-18843